FOR ORGANS, PIANOS & ELECTRONIC KEYBOARDS

E-Z PLAY TODAY

229

SONGS OF THE 30's

THE DECADE SERIES

E-Z Play TODAY chord notation is designed for playing **standard chord positions** or **single key chords** on all **major brand organs** and **electronic keyboards.**

Contents

10 All Of Me
12 Blue Prelude
14 Boo-Hoo
16 Bye Bye Blues
18 Continental, The
22 East Of The Sun (And West Of The Moon)
24 Easy To Love
26 Falling In Love With Love
28 Foggy Day, A
30 For All We Know
32 Harbor Lights
34 Have You Ever Been Lonely?
36 Heartaches
38 I Can't Get Started
40 I Don't Know Why (I Just Do)
42 I'll Never Smile Again
44 I'm Gonna Sit Right Down And Write Myself A Letter
46 I've Got The World On A String
48 I've Got You Under My Skin
52 In A Shanty In Old Shanty Town
54 In The Mood
56 In The Still Of The Night
60 It Ain't Necessarily So
64 It's A Blue World
70 It's De-Lovely
72 It's Only A Paper Moon
74 It's The Talk Of The Town
76 Lady Is A Tramp, The
78 Let's Dance
80 Love Is Here To Stay

82 Love Letters In The Sand
84 Lullaby Of The Leaves
86 Memories Of You
88 Moon Over Miami
90 Moonglow
92 My Funny Valentine
94 My Prayer
96 Nevertheless (I'm In Love With You)
98 Nice Work If You Can Get It
100 On The Sunny Side Of The Street
102 Paper Doll
104 Pennies From Heaven
106 Red Sails In The Sunset
67 Say "Si, Si"
108 September Song
110 Smoke Gets In Your Eyes
112 Some Day My Prince Will Come
114 Summertime
116 That's My Desire
118 These Foolish Things (Remind Me Of You)
120 They Can't Take That Away From Me
122 This Can't Be Love
124 Under A Blanket Of Blue
126 What A Diff'rence A Day Made
128 Where Or When
130 Where The Blue Of The Night (Meets The Gold Of The Day)
132 You're My Everything
134 Yours

136 Registration Guide

HAL•LEONARD CORPORATIC

7777 W. BLUEMOUND RD. P.O. BOX 13819 MILWAUKEE, WI 5.

D1451446

THE THIRTIES

by Stanley Green

HINDENBURG EXPLODES

33 Killed, 64 Saved in Lakehurst Blas

*I*f ever a decade needed songs to lift its spirits and send it spinning merrily across a dance floor, that decade was the Thirties. From the Wall Street crash to the outbreak of World War II, it was a period marked by the Great Depression at home and darkening war clouds abroad. This, then, was the era of soup kitchens, breadlines and bank failures, of bonus marchers and dust storms, of painful labor gains and rampant lawless gangs. Overseas, a far more menacing form of rampant lawlessness was evident. Under Nazi Führer Adolf Hitler, German troops occupied the Rhineland and scooped up Austria and Czechoslovakia. Under Fascist Duce Benito Mussolini, Italian forces subdued Ethiopia and Albania. Under the Japanese war lords, soldiers of the Empire of the Rising Sun subjugated Manchuria and other vast areas of China. At the decade's end, when Hitler and Soviet dictator Joseph Stalin agreed to carve up Poland between them, virtually the entire planet was plunged into the havoc of the most devastating conflict in history.

Adolph Hitler driving into Austria

𝒯he Thirties also had its share of other tragic headlines to take people's minds off their own imminent and potential troubles. In 1932, the 19-month-old baby of aviation ace Charles Lindbergh and Anne Morrow Lindbergh was kidnapped and murdered. In 1934, the S. S. Morro Castle went down in flames near Asbury Park, New Jersey, with a loss of over 125 lives. In 1937, the zeppelin Hindenburg, the world's largest dirigible, crashed on landing at Lakehurst, New Jersey, with a loss of 33 lives. No event, however, so intrigued a gossip-hungry public than the decision, in 1936, of Britain's King Edward VIII to abdicate the throne to marry American divorcée Wallis Warfield Simpson.

'I Am David Windsor'

𝓑ut despite roadblocks, it was still possible in the Thirties for people to cross over to the sunny side of the street. Prohibition was repealed. Franklin D. Roosevelt was in the White House energizing a dispirited nation with his alphabetical New Deal programs (NRA, CCC, PWA, WPA) and his broadcast fireside chats. Gable, Crawford, Garbo, and Shirley Temple were on the silver screen, Joe Louis was in the ring, Lou Gehrig was up at bat, "Wrong-Way" Corrigan was up in the air, and the Dionne Quintuplets were in their bassinets. The period also had its share of nonsense in the form of goldfish swallowing, zoot suits, and the game of knock-knock. ("Knock-knock." "Who's there?" "Machiavelli." "Machiavelli who?" "Machiavelli good suit for $40.")

Roosevelt and His First Cabinet

As far as music was concerned, the Thirties was the decade of the big bands. They could be sweet or swingy, tasteful or gimmicky, but each orchestra had its own distinctive sound and style. Tootling a clarinet (like Benny Goodman and Artie Shaw), or blowing through a trombone (like Tommy Dorsey and Glenn Miller), or just waving a stick (like Guy Lombardo and Sammy Kaye), the band leaders were latter-day Pied Pipers luring millions into dance halls, movie palaces, nightclubs, and college proms. Even unseen — thanks to radio and recordings — they moved right into the nation's parlors and bedrooms, generating a musical excitement that did much to help people escape from the seemingly unmanagable conditions of the world.

And what an array of personalities and songs there were. Offering "The Sweetest Music This Side of Heaven," Guy Lombardo and his Royal Canadians were on hand to bounce through the tearstained cry of the spurned lover called "Boo-Hoo," or to glide along to the beat of "Heartaches." Nasal-voiced Rudy Vallee and his Connecticut Yankees managed to sail

smoothly through the misty "Harbor Lights." Glen Gray and the Casa Loma Orchestra — with Sonny Dunham on trumpet — could be heard recalling fond "Memories of You." The languid romantic appeal of the South, both astral and lunar, was captured by the orchestras of Jack Teagarden in "Stars Fell on Alabama" and Ted Fiorito in "Moon Over Miami." Another "moon" song — "Moonglow" — was written by bandleaders Will Hudson and Eddie DeLange as a specialty for their own Hudson-DeLange Orchestra. Songs of foreign origin also won favor in the Thirties when introduced in the United States by leading dance bands. From France came "Avant de Mourir," better known as "My Prayer," which was popularized by

Glenn Miller and His Orchestra

orchestra and "I Can't Get Started" (a show tune by Vernon Duke and Ira Gershwin) became both his theme and biggest selling record.

As the decade came to a close, Glenn Miller emerged with his orchestra and first resounding hit, "In the Mood." (Remember the windup with the members of the brass section facing in all directions as they repeated the riff over and over again?) Even closer to jazz roots were the orchestras of two composer-pianists, the exuberant Fats Waller (who did *not* compose his most popular number, "I'm Gonna Sit Right Down and Write Myself a Letter"), and the more urbane Duke Ellington (whose standards include "Caravan" and "Mood Indigo").

Cab Calloway

Sammy Kaye's Swing and Sway group; from Cuba, "Para Vego Me Voy," which became "Say Si Si" when it was brought over by rhumba maestro Xavier Cugat; and from Mexico, "Cuando Vuelva a Tu Lado" — or "What a Diff'rence a Day Made" — was identified with Richard Himber's Ritz-Carlton Orchestra.

*I*n 1934, Benny Goodman organized his first dance band and within two years had been proclaimed the undisputed King of Swing. Like every orchestra at the time, Goodman's had a theme song, the bright, crisp invitation, "Let's Dance." Another theme song, "I'm Getting Sentimental Over You," became the trade mark of that Sentimental Gentleman of Swing, Tommy Dorsey. Dorsey also had a resounding hit — with young Frank Sinatra on the vocals — when he introduced the threnodic "I'll Never Smile Again," penned by pianist Ruth Lowe in memory of her husband who had died within a year after their marriage. In 1937, Dorsey's star trumpeter, Bunny Berigan, left the band to front his own

IN THE MOOD

Words by
ANDY RAZAF

Music by
JOE GARLAND

Introduced by
GLENN MILLER

Democrats Elect 254, While
Republicans Obtain 84,
and Progressives 6.

By TURNER CATLEDGE
Republican hopes of making heavy inroads upon the huge Democratic majorities in Congress were apparently smothered under Roosevelt landslide.

fident that all of us Americans will now pull together for the common good. I send you every good wish."

UNION PARTY

President's Vote and Margin
Which Reached 1
Set Hi

DEMOCRATS

FINAL
Rain and much colder today. Tomorrow fair, with little change in temperature.
Temperatures Yesterday—Max., 75; Min., 44

The New York Times.

Copyright, 1936, by The New York Times Company.

"All the News That's
Fit to Print."

NEW YORK, WEDNESDAY, NOVEMBER 4, 1936.

TWO CENTS in New York City. | THREE CENTS Within 500 Miles | FOUR CENTS in 7th and 8th Postal

OL. LXXXVI.....No. 28,774.

ROOSEVELT SWEEPS THE NATION;
ELECTORAL VOTE EXCEEDS 500;
WINS; CHARTER ADOPTED

Comment
Today | LEHMAN VOTE CUT

POLL SETS REC

Roosevelt Elect
Vote of 519
as a Minim

NO SWING TO

Today

★ King Kept His Word.
★ He Live Happily.
★ Runyon's Rich Friend.

By ARTHUR BRISBANE

METROPOLITAN FORECAST

2 Full Pages of Pictures on Britain's Swift Moving Drama

New York American

CHARACTER QUALITY
AMERICA FIRST!
ENTERPRISE
AN AMERICAN PAPER FOR THE AMERICAN PEOPLE

No. 19,501—DAILY

FRIDAY, DECEMBER 11, 1936—44 PAGES

6 A.M.
FINAL

EDWARD'S FAREWELL TODAY
BROADCASTS AS 'DAVID WINDSOR';
TO BECOME GEORGE VI; WALLIS

INDUSTRY GIVES
U.S. ITS PLEDGE
TO CO-OPERATE

Manufacturers' Association Urges 'Era of Good Will,' Adopts Principles for 1937

Full co-oper

Baldwin's Famous
Victory

Only Mr. Eden's 51 to
in Ethiopia Co

'I Am David I

There is a growing realization that ethical and humanitarian considerations have a vital relation to economics.—Ida M. Tarbell

Boston Sunday Post

EXTRA

SUNDAY MORNING, MARCH 13, 1938

PRICE TEN CENTS

AGE INDEX TO FEATURES

SEVENTY TWO PAGES

Three Big Features
of the Sunday Post

HITLER DEFIES WORLD TO
TAKE AUSTRIA FROM HIM

MUST PICK OUT
JOB WITH CARE

People Limited in Field of

Tells Cheering Crowds That Return of Country to Germany Was His "Divine" Mission----Return
Triumphantly to Land of Birth and Soil He Left in 1912----Takes Control of Vienna Today
----Troops Swarm Into Austria by Land and Air----Wave of Arrests Follows Invasion

Czechoslovakia Masses Arm
Frontier; France Faces Cr

George Gershwin

The incredible appeal of the "talkies" did much to bring about the demise of vaudeville as the most popular form of mass entertainment. Songs, of course, quickly became a major attraction on the screen — whether they were sung by Ruby and Dick in backstage sagas, Fred and Ginger in glossy comic escapades, or Jeanette and Nelson in romantic costume epics. These musicals called upon the services of the top talent of both Hollywood and Broadway. In 1934, "The Continental," by Con Conrad and Herb Magidson, was introduced in the Astaire-Rogers vehicle *The Gay Divorcee* and became the first song to win an Academy Award. Three years later, George and Ira Gershwin contributed the score for the team's seventh movie, *Shall We Dance,* in which Fred sang the rueful admission "They Can't Take That Away From Me." The songwriting brothers followed up that movie with *A Damsel in Distress,* Astaire's first solo starring movie, whence came "Nice Work if You Can Get It" and "A Foggy Day." The last song George Gershwin wrote before his untimely death at the age of 38 was "Love Is Here to Stay," included in his score for *The*

Goldwyn Follies. Another major figure of the American musical theatre was Cole Porter, who wrote both music and lyrics for two Hollywood spectacles of 1936 — *Born to Dance,* which introduced "Easy to Love" (sung by James Stewart to Eleanor Powell), and *Rosalie,* which introduced "In the Still of the Night" (sung by Nelson Eddy to Eleanor Powell).

The most popular singing idol of the screen, however, was the former Paul Whiteman vocalist, Bing Crosby, who casually crooned his way through 24 movies during the decade. One of these, *Pennies from Heaven,* gave us a title song that philosophically urged the acceptance of bad times in order to be able to enjoy good times ("If you want the things you love, you must have showers"). On the technical front, surely among the great innovations in the art of the cinema was *Snow White and the Seven Dwarfs,* Walt Disney's first full-length animated cartoon, whose score included the poignant "Someday My Prince Will Come."

Fred Astaire

After rapid growth in the Twenties, radio became the major provider of home entertainment in the Thirties. The coverage was now broad enough to include news events, comedy programs (Jack Benny, Amos and Andy), dramas (in 1938, Orson Welles scared the pants off gullible listeners with his dramatization of H. G. Wells' *The War of the Worlds*), and musical variety shows. Among those whose voices introduced and popularized songs over the air were Bing Crosby (singing his theme "Where the Blue of the Night Meets the Gold of the Day"), dynamic Belle Baker ("All of Me"), Irish tenor Morton Downey ("For All We Know"), and Crosby's chief crooning rivals, Rudy Vallee ("Nevertheless") and Russ Columbo ("Love Letters in the Sand").

The Broadway theatre of the Thirties, though hardly as robust as it had been during the halcyon days of the previous decade, still managed to offer many successful shows and durable songs. And once again it was blessed by contributions from the giants of American music — Jerome Kern, Irving Berlin, George Gershwin, Richard Rodgers, and Cole Porter. Kern, generally acknowledged as the father of musical comedy joined lyricist Otto Harbach to provide a rich, melodic score for *Roberta,* including the brooding torch ballad "Smoke Gets in Your Eyes." In 1935, Gershwin, in collaboration with his brother Ira and DuBose Heyward, created the classic folk opera, *Porgy and Bess,* in which the plaintive lullaby "Summertime" was first heard. After spending over two years in Hollywood, Rodgers and his partner Lorenz Hart returned to Broadway in the mid-Thirties for a succession of hits such as *Babes in Arms,* featuring "The Lady Is a Tramp," "Where or When," and "My Funny Valentine," and *The Boys from Syracuse,* featuring "Falling in Love With Love" and "This Can't Be Love." And Porter continued

Tamara Sings "Smoke Gets In Your Eyes"

Jerome Kern

Richard Rodgers and Lorenz Hart

to transport audiences into his own glittering, carefree world with a total of nine musicals, including *Red, Hot and Blue!* In that one, Ethel Merman and Bob Hope sang the duet "It's DeLovely," relating the story of a girl and boy from the night they fall in love, through their wedding and honeymoon, and up to the birth of their first born.

Joining the ranks of Broadway masters in the Thirties was Kurt Weill, a victim of Hitler's Germany, who quickly became a leader in expanding the horizons of the commercial musical theatre. Weill's second Broadway show, *Knickerbocker Holiday*, written with Maxwell Anderson, not only provided Walter Huston (as Pieter Stuyvesant) with the memorable "September Song," it also showed deep concern for the vital issue of freedom versus totalitarianism. This, in fact, was the issue that — on September 3, 1939 — at last rallied the European democracies to strike back at Hitler's aggression. Only twenty years after "the war to end war," another even more horrible carnage had begun.

Walter Huston as Pieter Stuyvesant

Kurt Weill

Ethel Merman and Bob Hope in "Red, Hot and Blue!"

All Of Me

Registration 4
Rhythm: Fox Trot or Swing - 140

Words and Music by
Seymour Simons and Gerald Marks

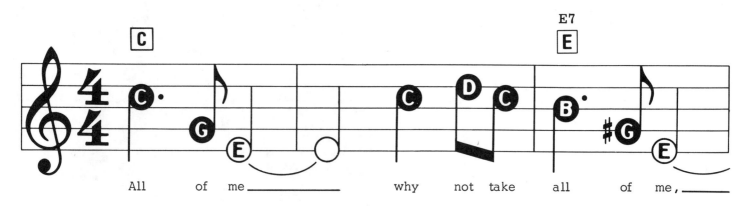

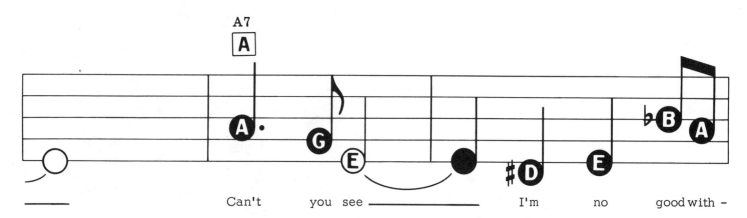

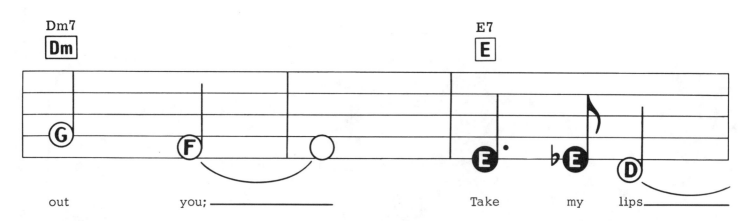

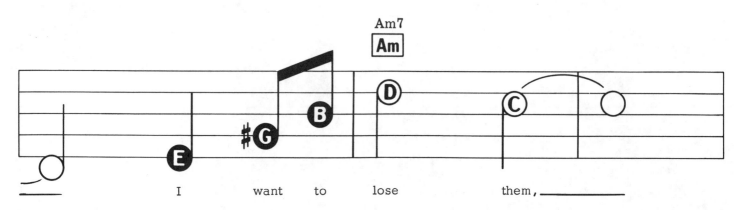

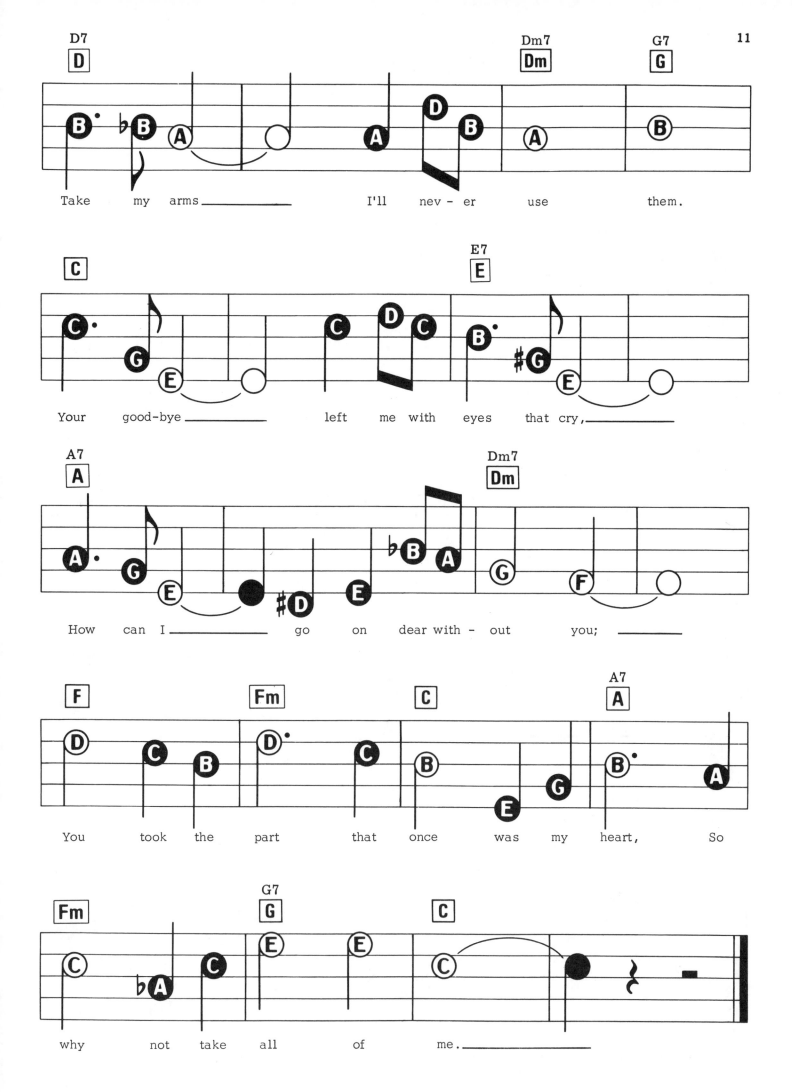

Blue Prelude

Registration 5
Rhythm: Fox Trot or Swing ♩=130

Words by Gordon Jenkins
Music by Joe Bishop

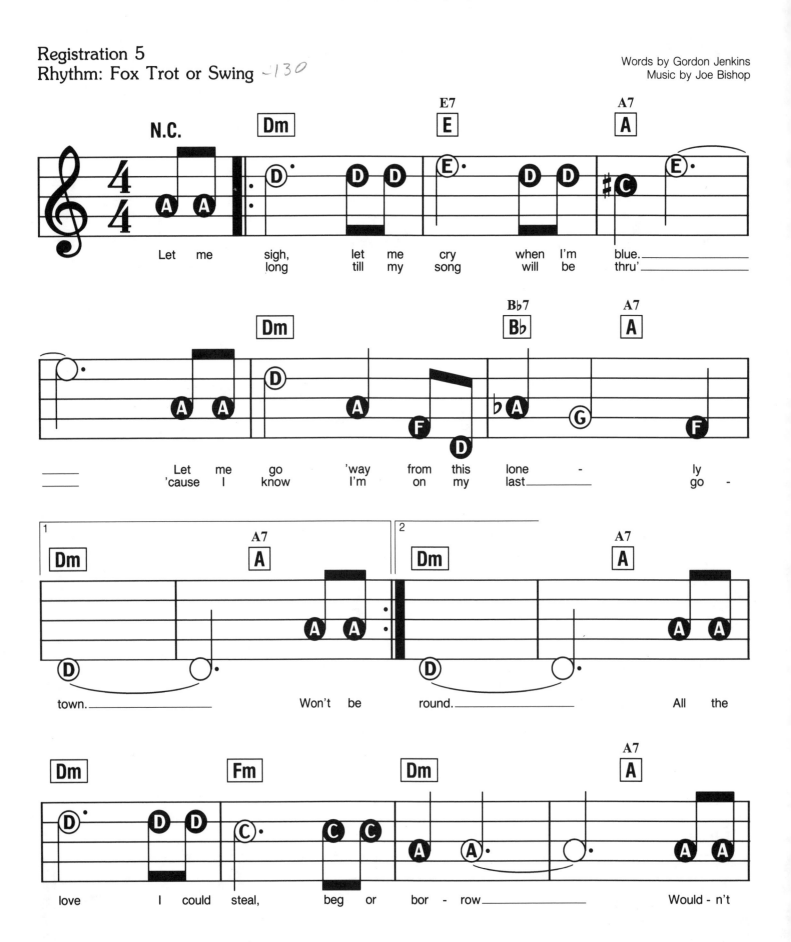

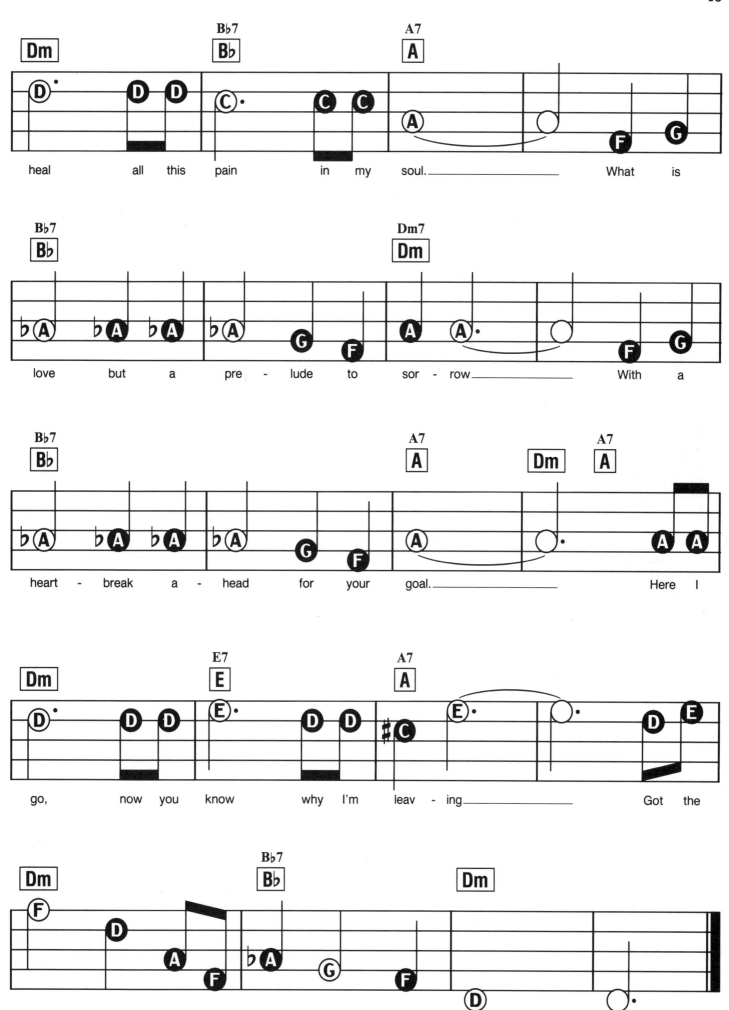

Dm Bb7 Bb A7 A
heal all this pain in my soul. What is
Bb7 Bb Dm7 Dm
love but a pre - lude to sor - row With a
Bb7 Bb A7 A Dm A7 A
heart - break a - head for your goal. Here I
Dm E7 E A7 A
go, now you know why I'm leav - ing Got the
Dm Bb7 Bb Dm
blues, what can I lose, good - bye.

Boo-Hoo

Registration 10
Rhythm: Swing or Jazz - 140

Words and Music by Edward Heyman,
Carmen Lombardo and John Jacob Loeb

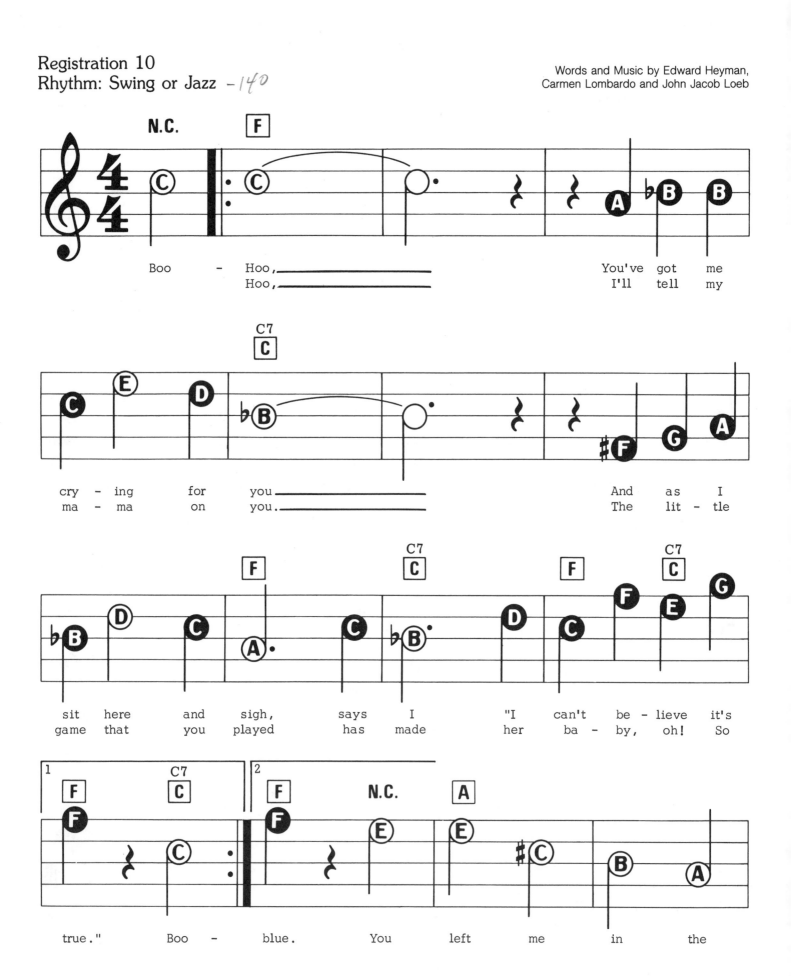

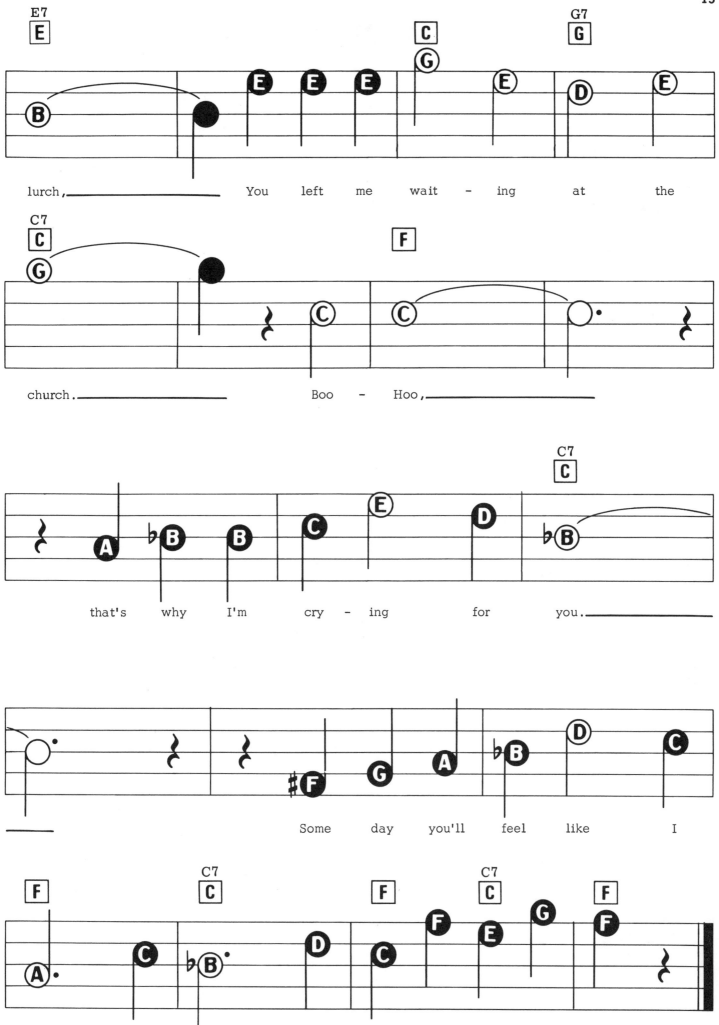

Bye Bye Blues

Registration 5
Rhythm: Fox Trot - 140

Words and Music by Fred Hamm, Dave Bennett,
Bert Town, and Chauncey Gray

Bye   bye   blues

Bye   bye   blues

Bells   ring,   Birds

sing   Sun   is   shin - ing,

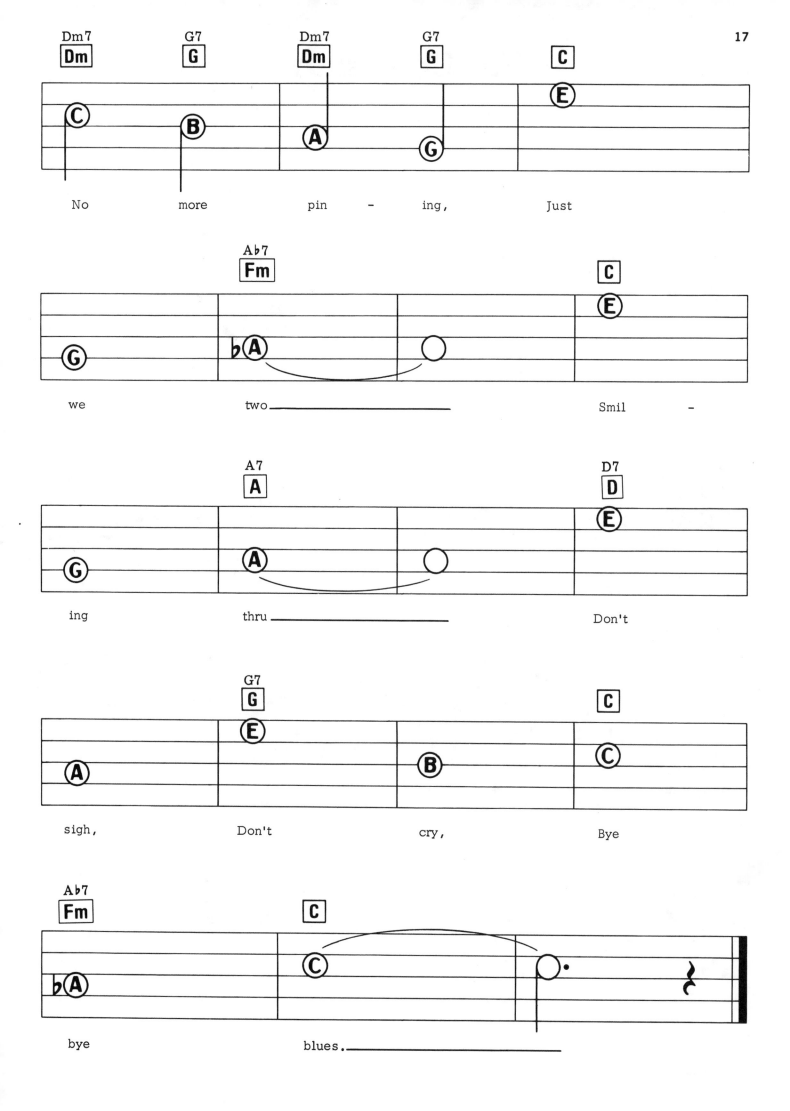

The Continental

Registration 5
Rhythm: Samba or Latin

Words by Con Conrad
Music by Herbert Magidson

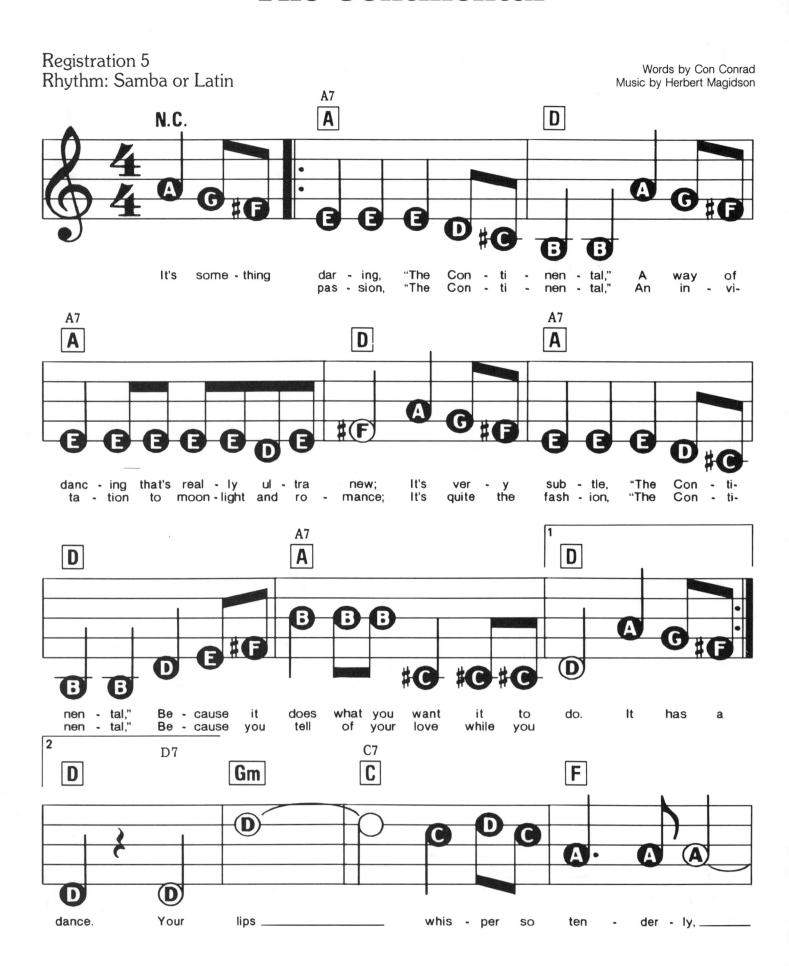

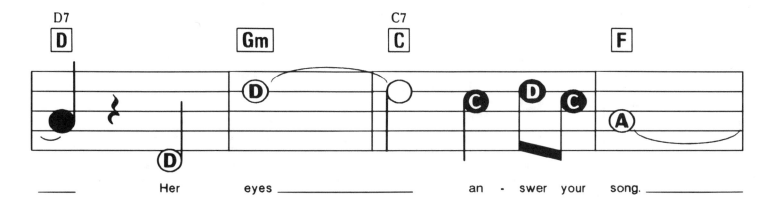

Her eyes _____ an - swer your song. _____

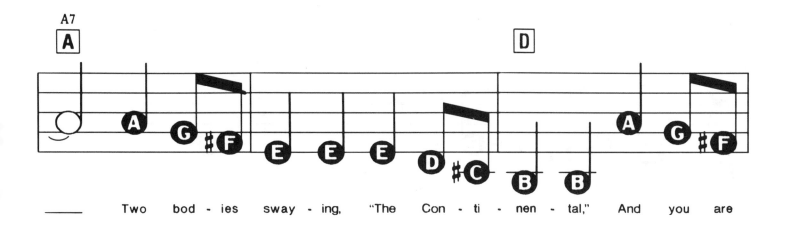

_____ Two bod - ies sway - ing, "The Con - ti - nen - tal," And you are

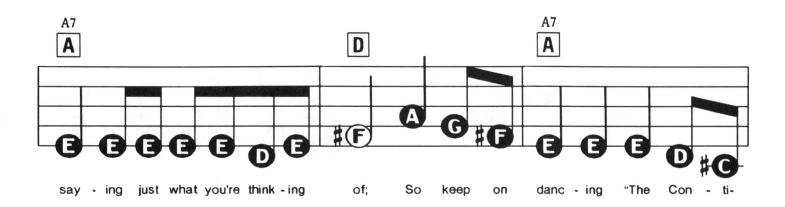

say - ing just what you're think - ing of; So keep on danc - ing "The Con - ti-

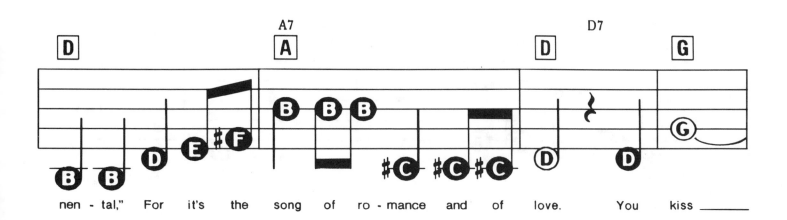

nen - tal," For it's the song of ro - mance and of love. You kiss _____

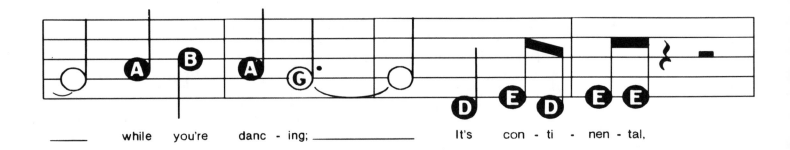

while you're danc - ing; _____ It's con - ti - nen - tal,

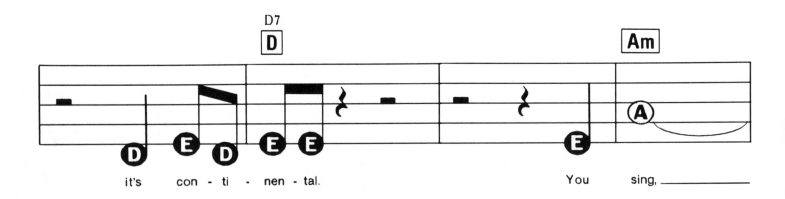

it's con - ti - nen - tal. You sing, _____

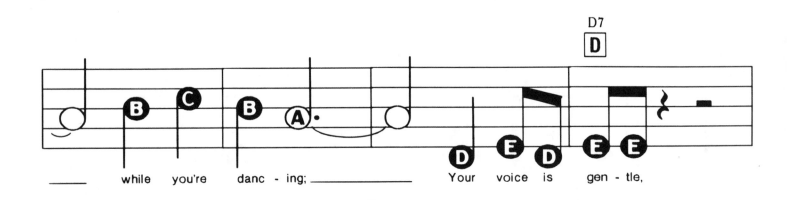

while you're danc - ing; _____ Your voice is gen - tle,

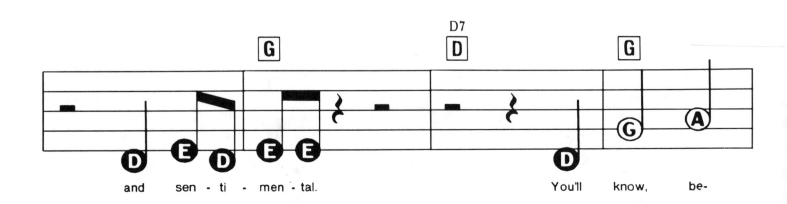

and sen - ti - men - tal. You'll know, be-

21

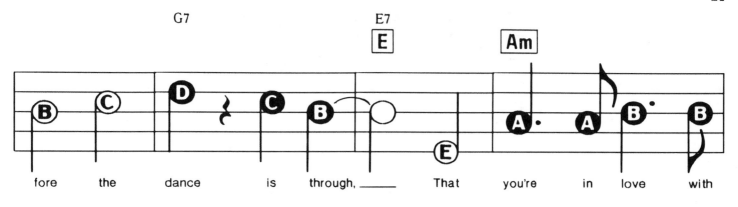

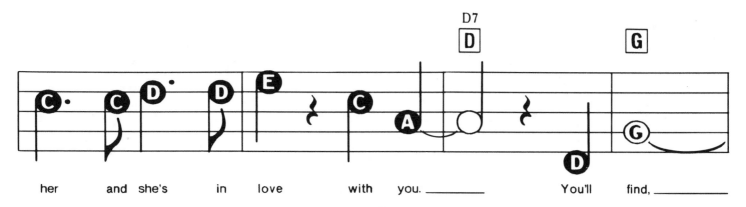

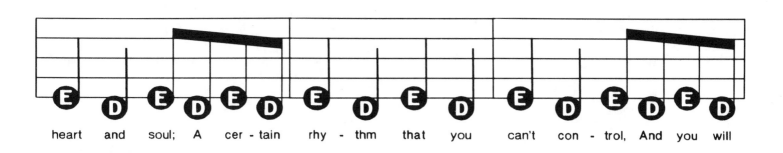

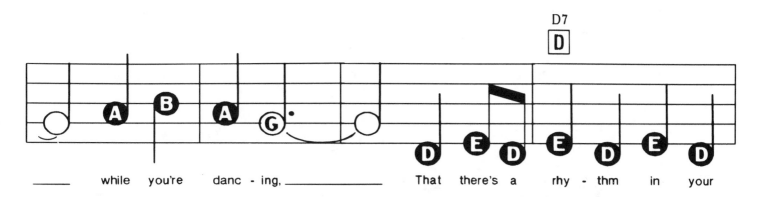

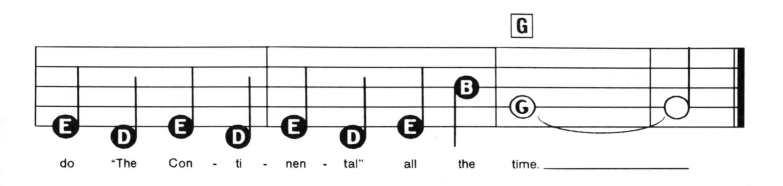

East Of The Sun
(And West Of The Moon)

Registration 9
Rhythm: Swing or Jazz —120

Words and Music by
Brooks Bowman

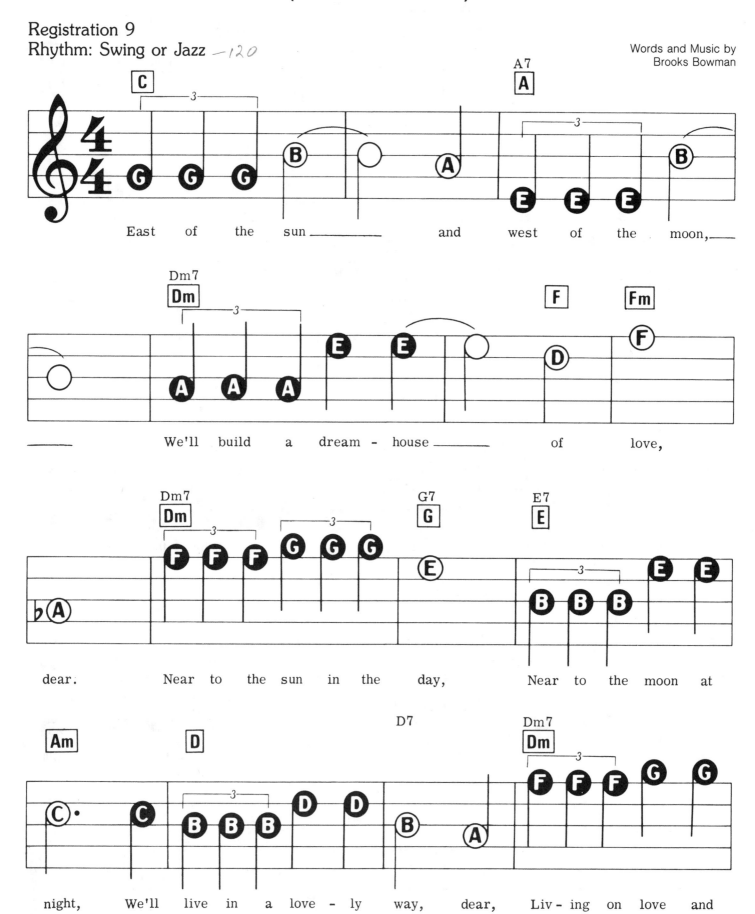

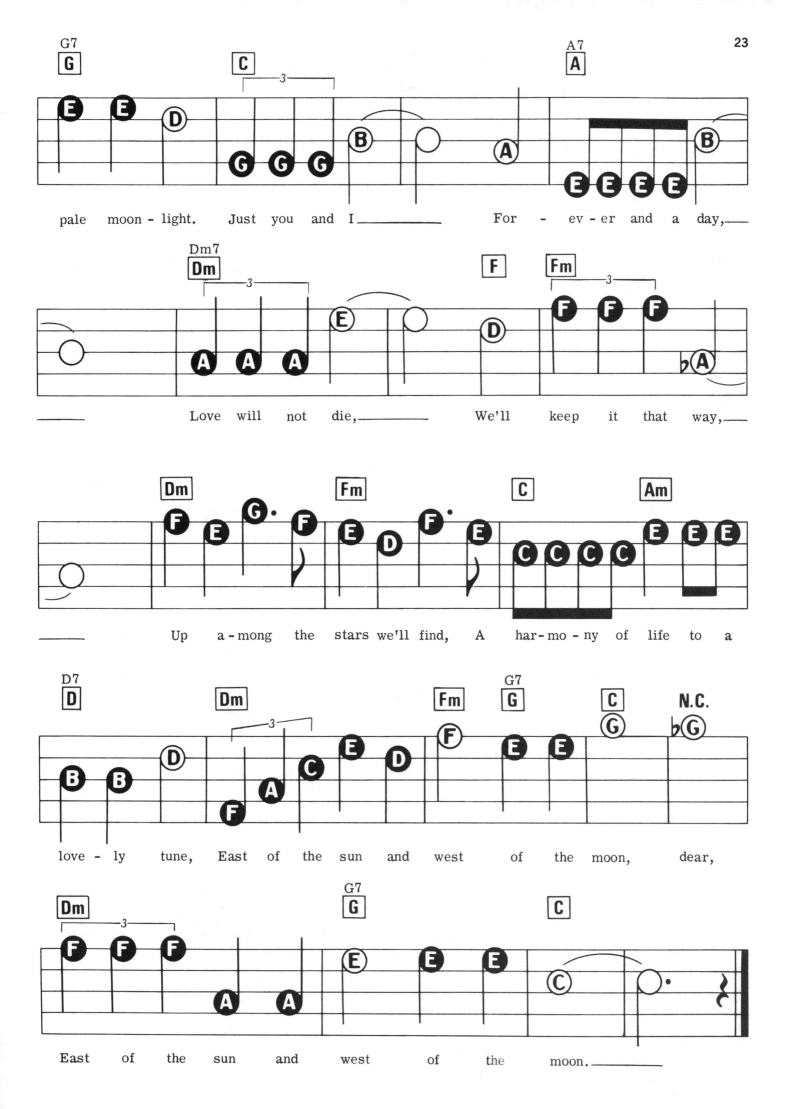

Easy To Love

(From "BORN TO DANCE")

Registration 3
Rhythm: Swing or Fox Trot — 130

Words and Music by
Cole Porter

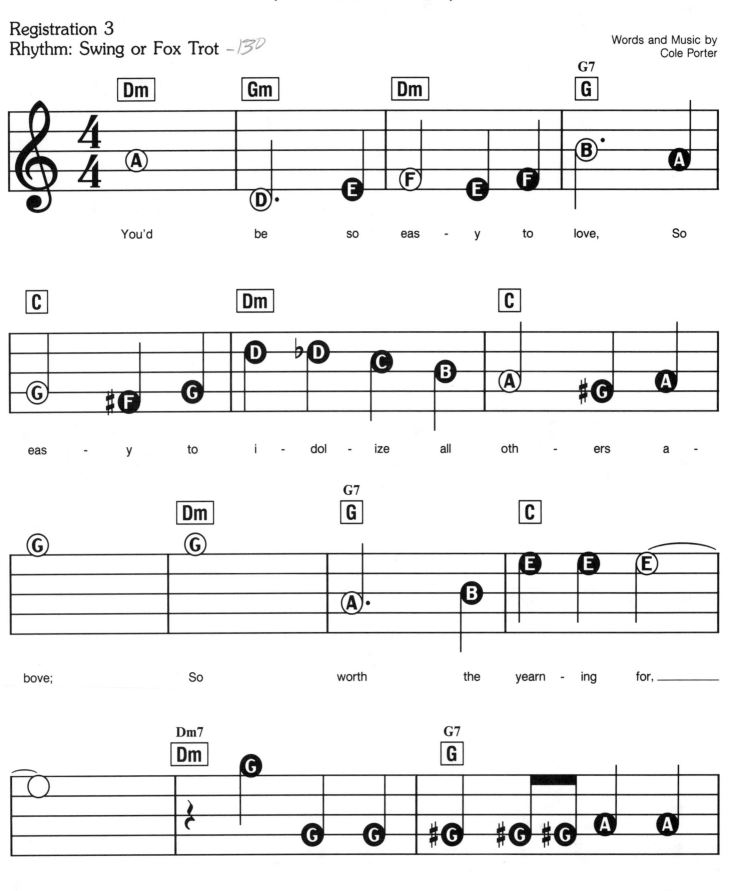

You'd be so eas - y to love, So

eas - y to i - dol - ize all oth - ers a -

bove; So worth the yearn - ing for, _____

_____ So swell to keep ev - 'ry home - fire

25

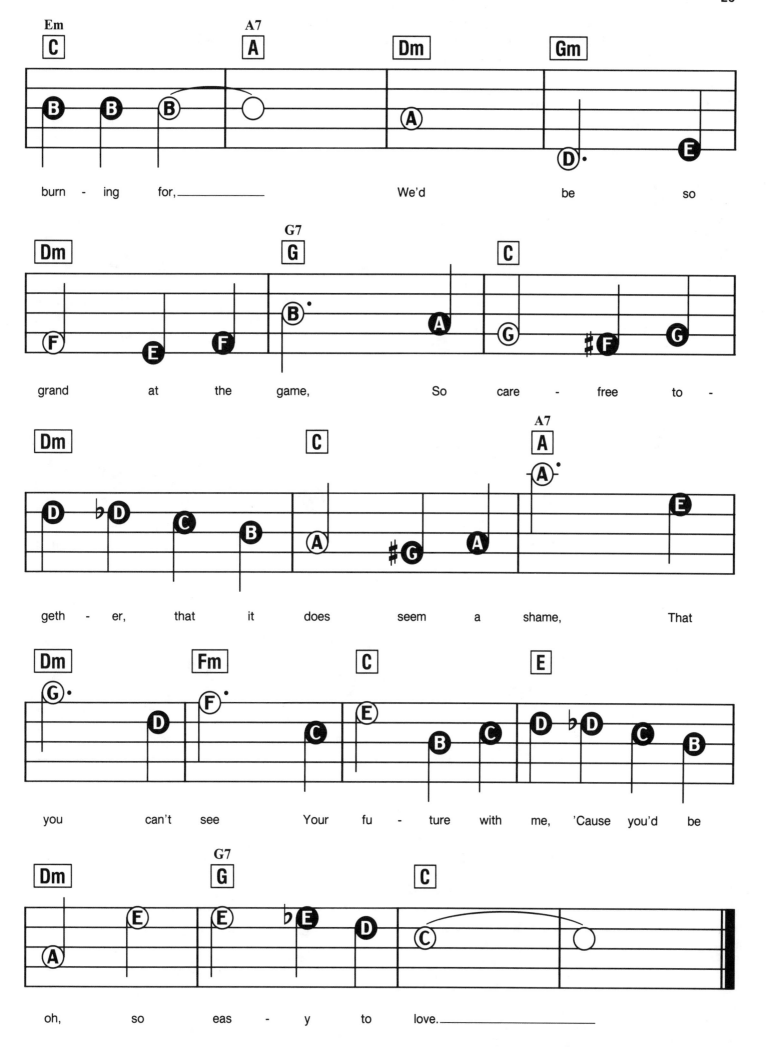

Falling In Love With Love

(From "THE BOYS FROM SYRACUSE")

Registration 5
Rhythm: Waltz ♩=136

Words by Lorenz Hart
Music by Richard Rodgers

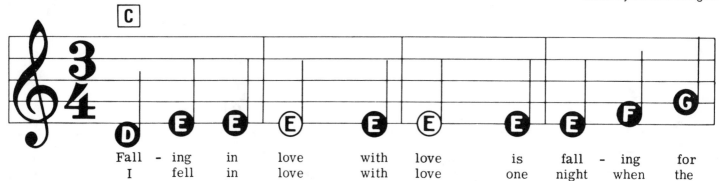

Fall - ing in love with love is fall - ing for
I fell in love with with love one night when for the

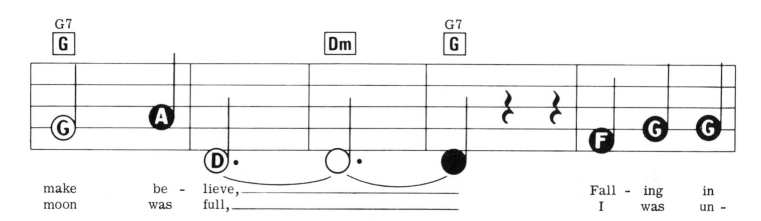

make be - lieve,_____ Fall - ing in
moon was full,_____ I was un -

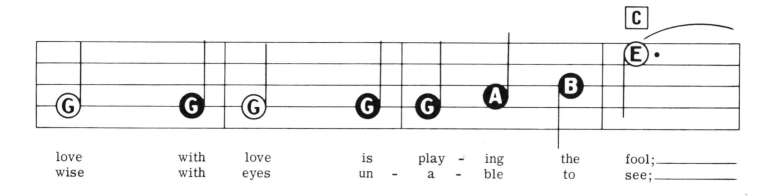

love with love is play - ing the fool;_____
wise with eyes un - a - ble to see;_____

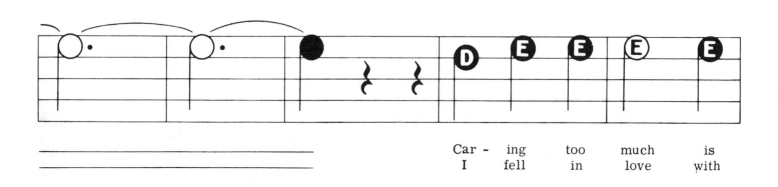

_____ Car - ing too much is
_____ I fell in love with

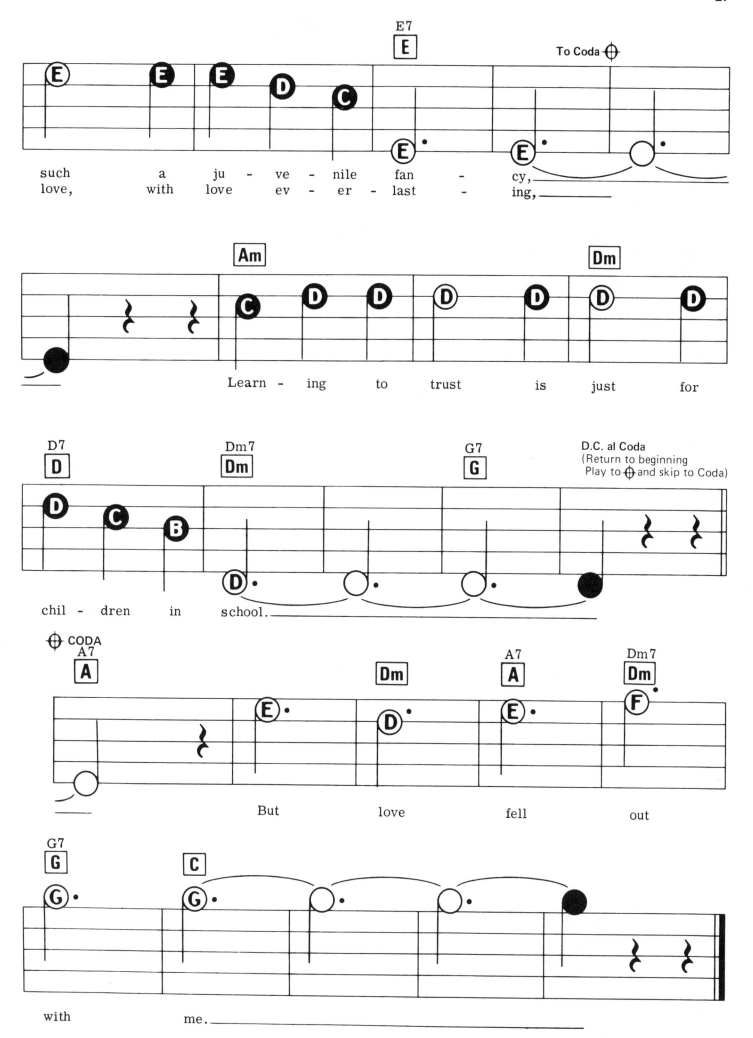

A Foggy Day
(From "A Damsel In Distress")

Registration 5
Rhythm: Swing or Fox Trot - 130

Words by Ira Gershwin
Music by George Gershwin

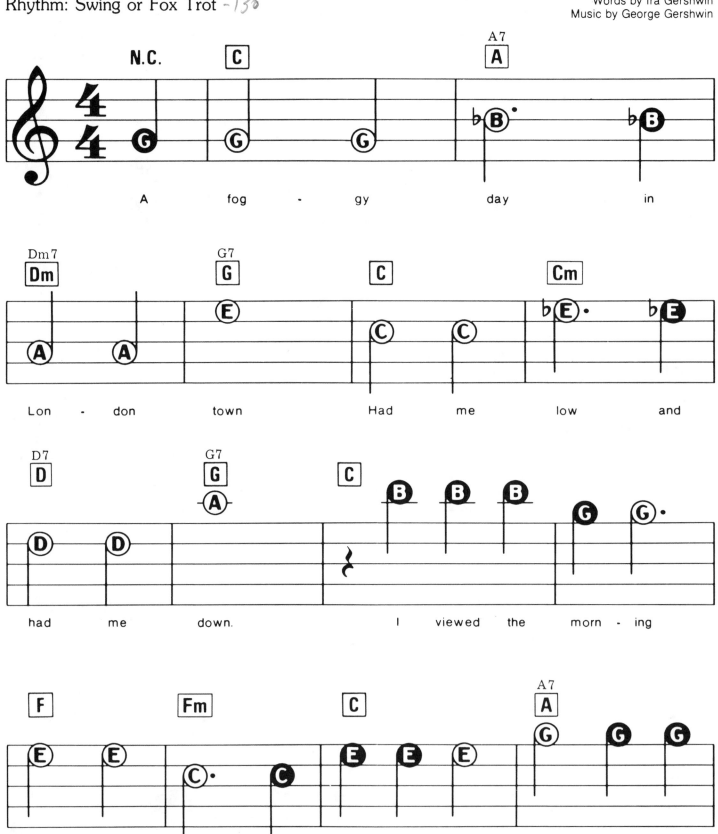

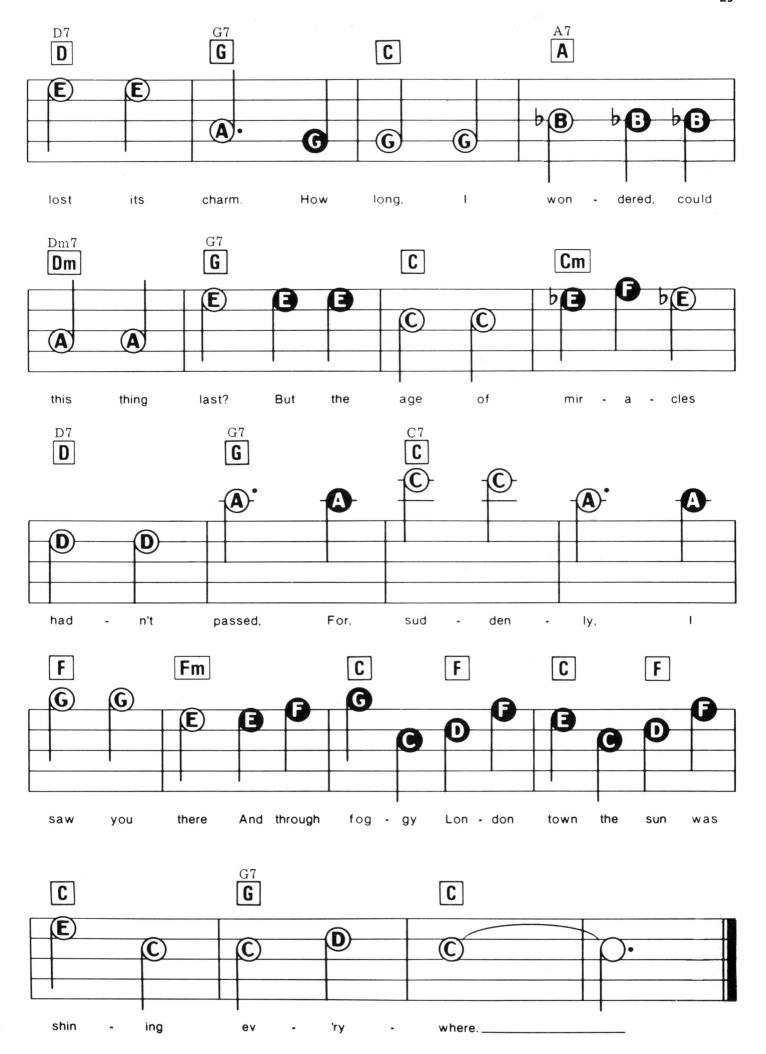

For All We Know

Registration 1
Rhythm: Swing

Words by Sam M. Lewis
Music by J. Fred Coots

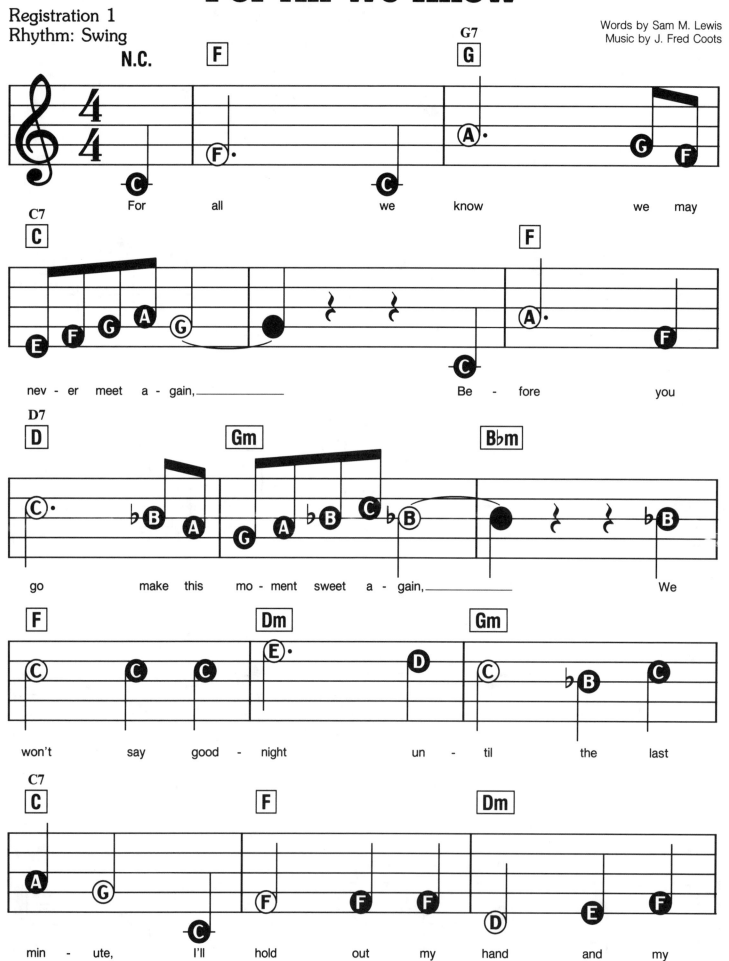

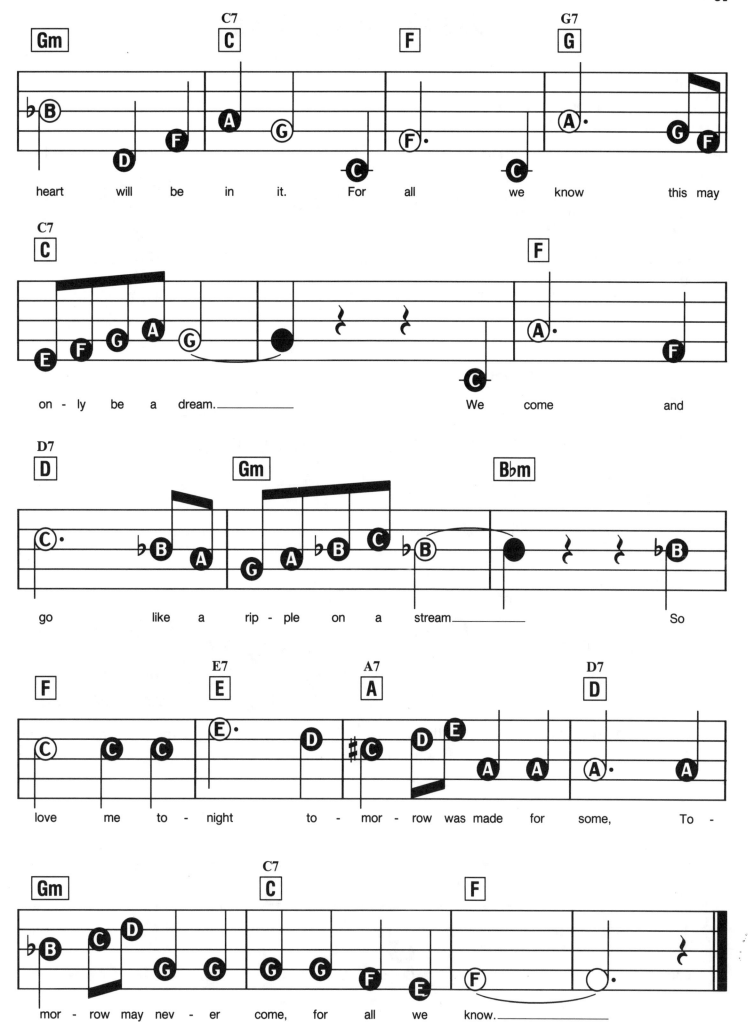

Harbor Lights

Registration 4
Rhythm: Fox Trot or Swing

Words and Music by
Jimmy Kennedy and Hugh Williams

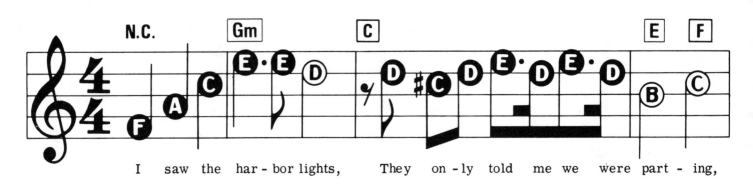

I saw the har - bor lights, They on - ly told me we were part - ing,

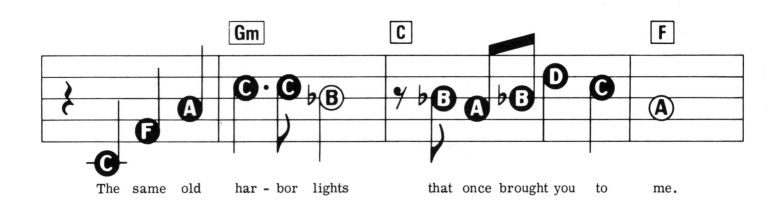

The same old har - bor lights that once brought you to me.

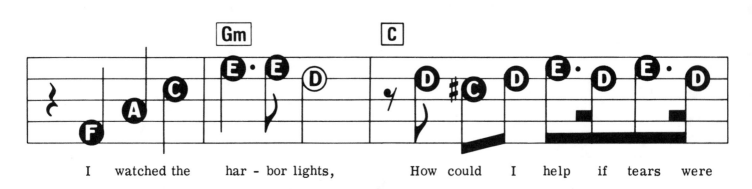

I watched the har - bor lights, How could I help if tears were

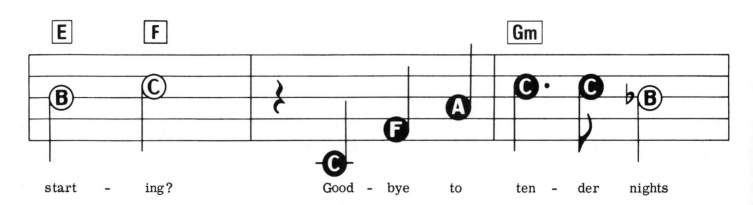

start - ing? Good - bye to ten - der nights

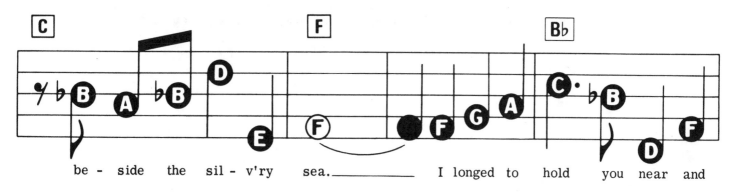

be - side the sil - v'ry sea._____ I longed to hold you near and

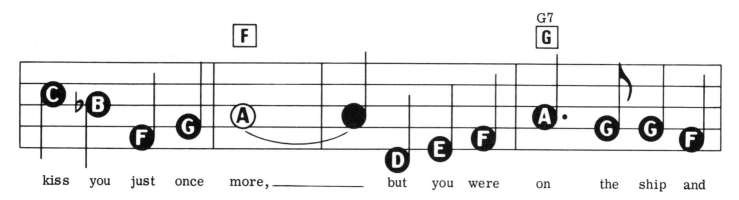

kiss you just once more,_____ but you were on the ship and

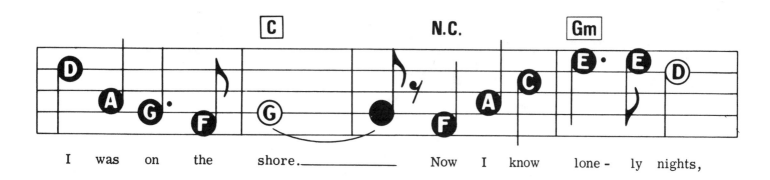

I was on the shore._____ Now I know lone - ly nights,

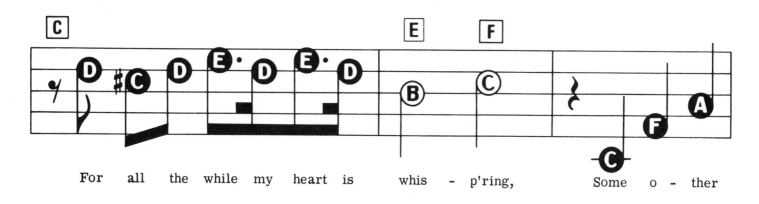

For all the while my heart is whis - p'ring, Some o - ther

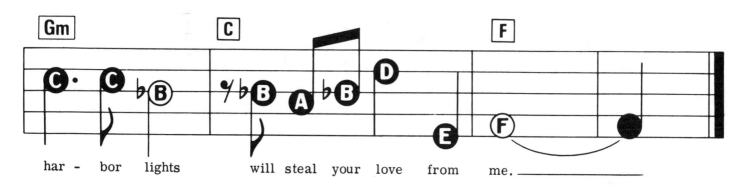

har - bor lights will steal your love from me._____

Have You Ever Been Lonely?
(Have You Ever Been Blue?)

Registration 3
Rhythm: Swing or Jazz

Words by George Brown
Music by Peter DeRose

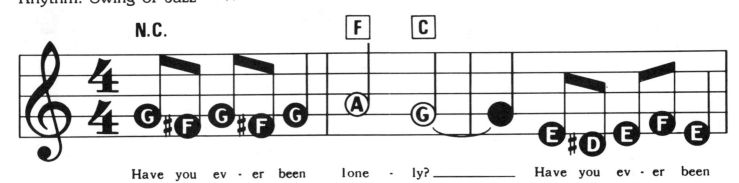

Have you ev-er been lone-ly? _____ Have you ev-er been

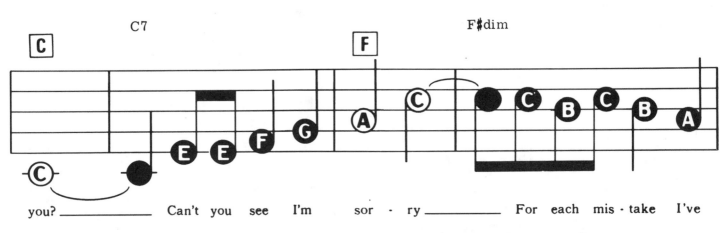

blue? _____ Have you ev-er loved some-one _____ Just as I love

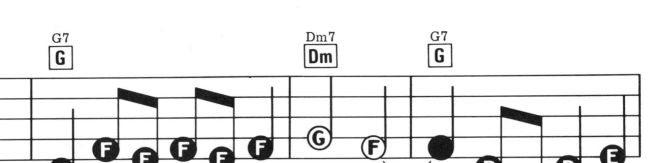

you? _____ Can't you see I'm sor-ry _____ For each mis-take I've

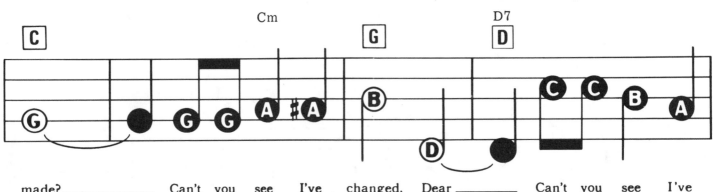

made? _____ Can't you see I've changed, Dear _____ Can't you see I've

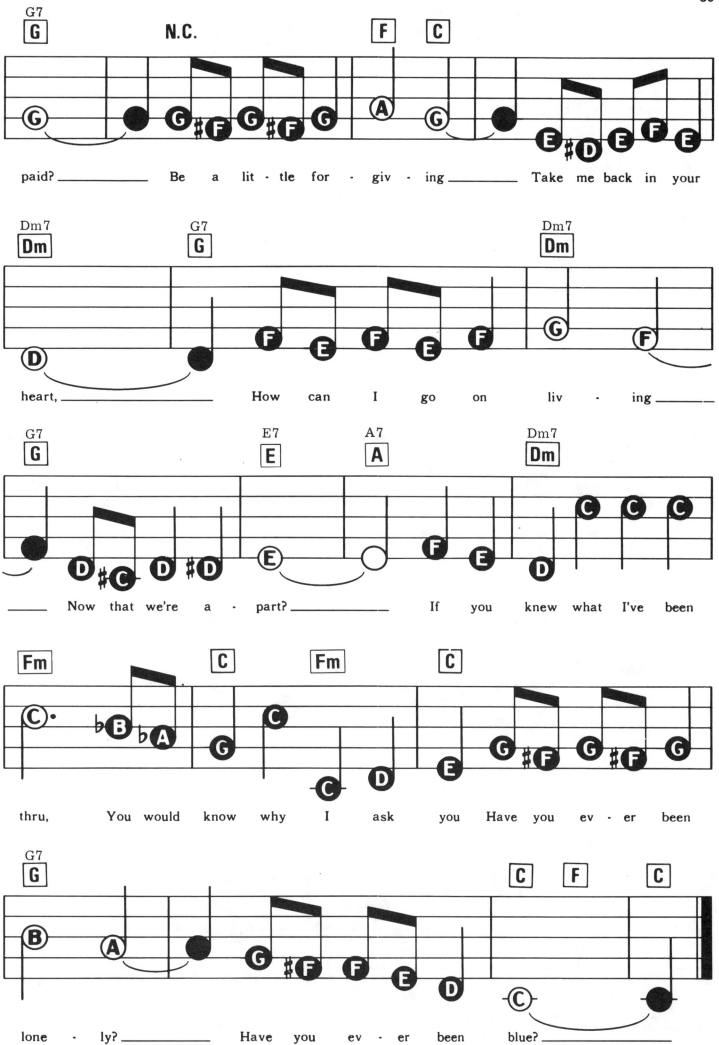

Heartaches

Registration 4
Rhythm: Fox Trot or Swing -130

Words by John Klenner
Music by Al Hoffman

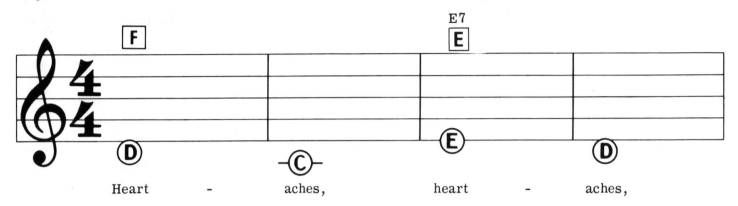

Heart - aches, heart - aches,

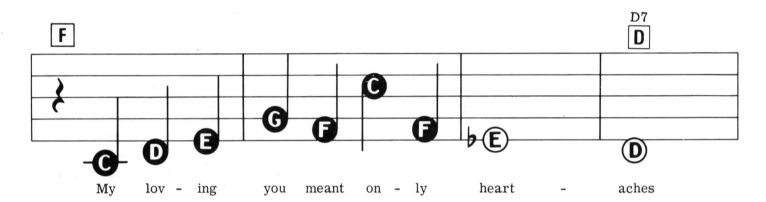

My lov - ing you meant on - ly heart - aches

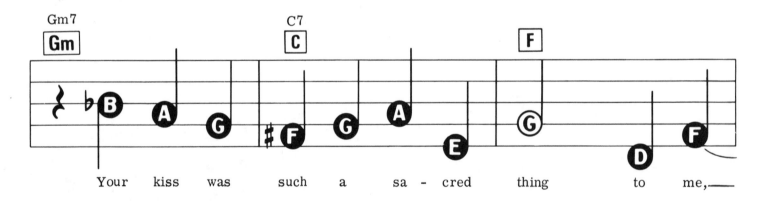

Your kiss was such a sa - cred thing to me,

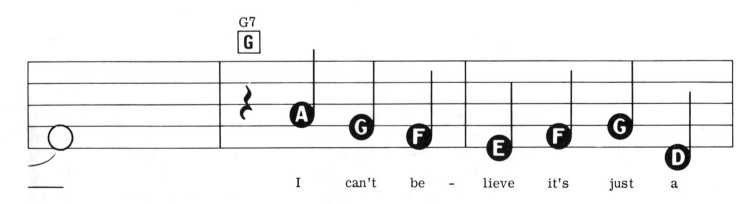

I can't be - lieve it's just a

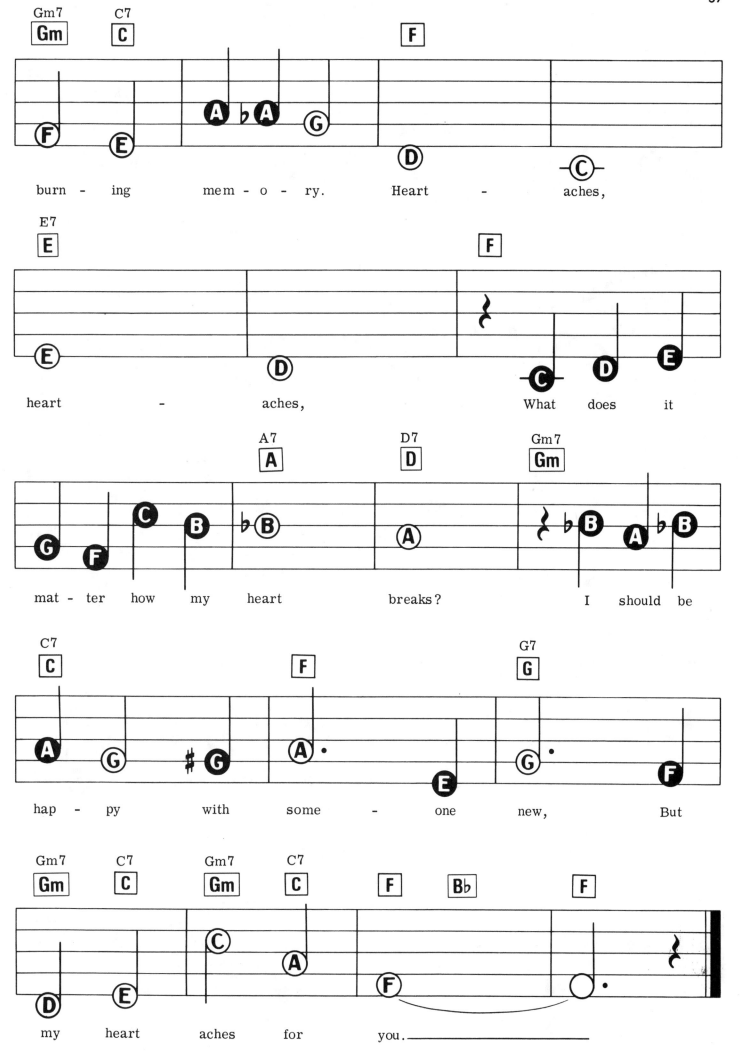

I Can't Get Started

Registration 2
Rhythm: Swing or Jazz

Fox T. & V
90

Words by Ira Gershwin
Music by Vernon Duke

I've flown a - round the world in a plane; _____ I've set - tled
hun - dred yards in ten flat; _____ The Prince of

re - vo - lu - tions in Spain; The North Pole I have char - ted, But can't get start - ed with
Wales has cop - ied my hat; With queens I've 'a la cart - ed, But can't get start - ed with

you. _____ A - round a golf course I'm un - der par, _____ And all the
you. _____ The lead - ing tail - ors fol - low my styles, _____ And tooth - paste

mov - ies want me to star; I've got a house a show - place, But
ads all fea - ture my smiles; The As - tor - bilts I vis - it, But

I get no - place with you. You're so su - preme,
say, what IS it with you? When first we met,

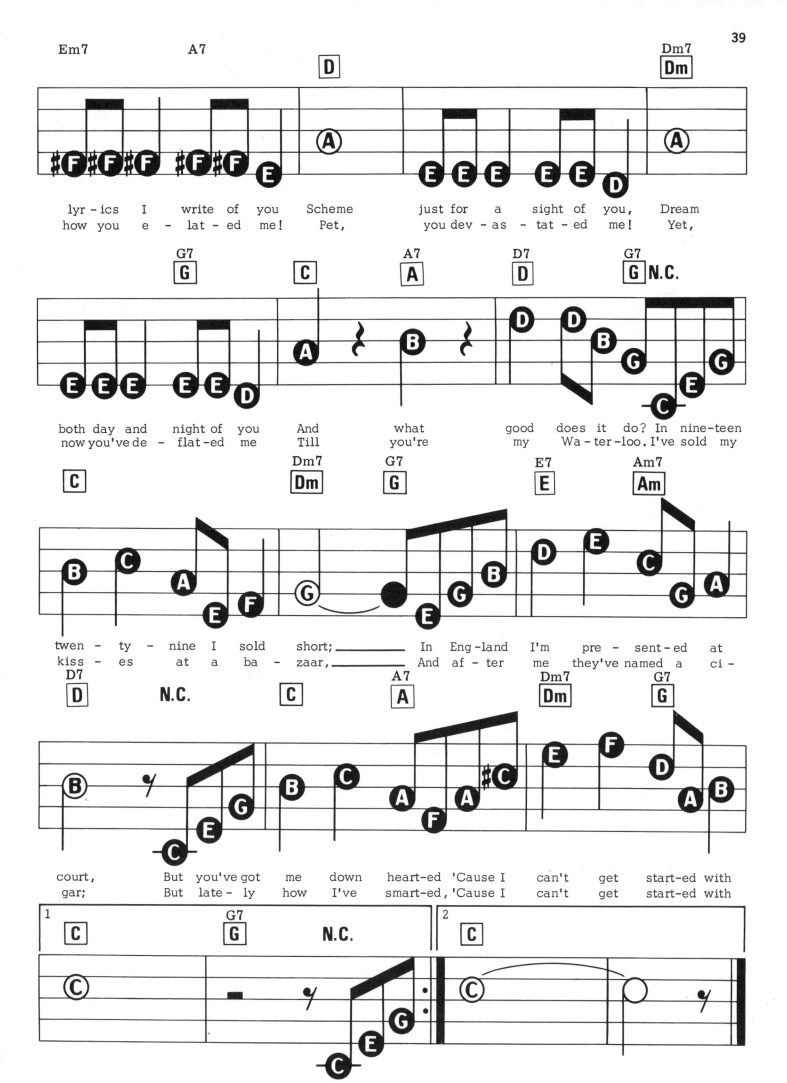

I Don't Know Why
(I Just Do)

Registration 8
Rhythm: Fox Trot or Swing ♩06+

Words by Roy Turk
Music by Fred E. Ahlert

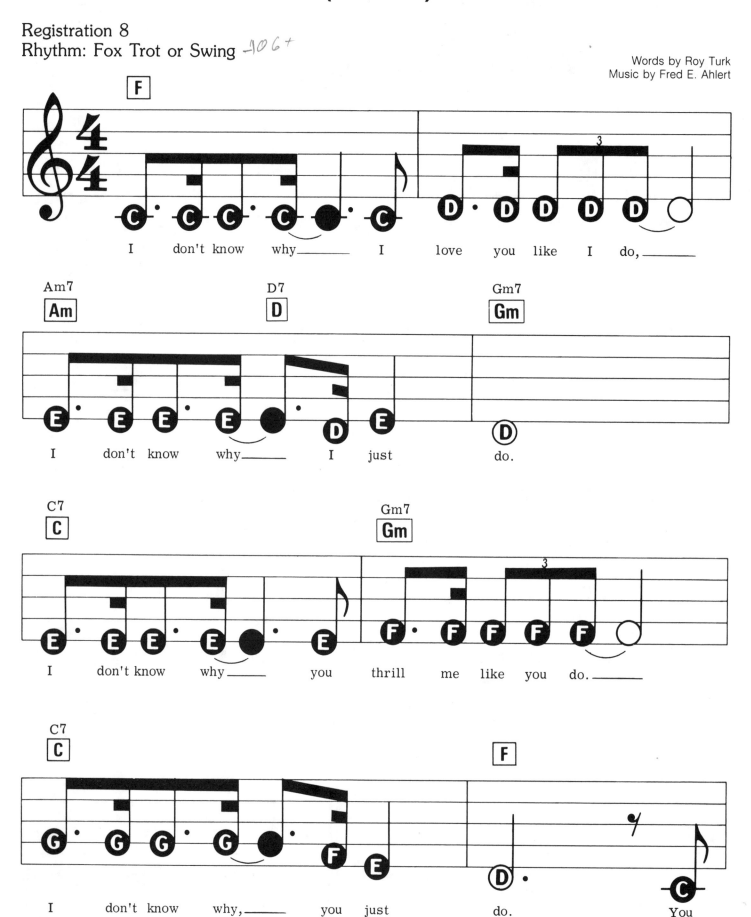

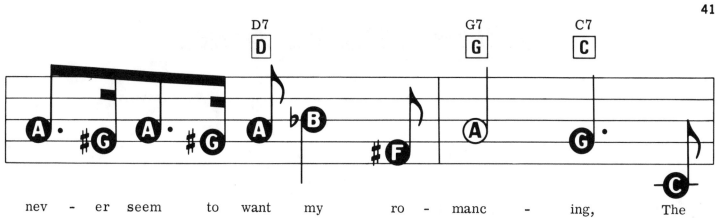

nev - er seem to want my ro - manc - ing, The

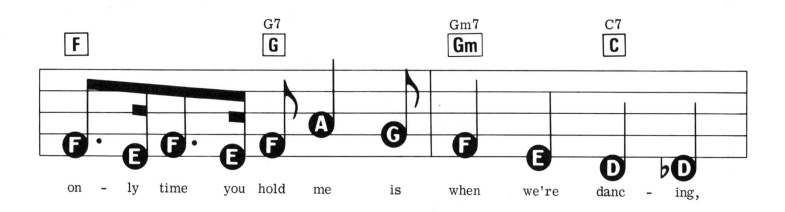

on - ly time you hold me is when we're danc - ing,

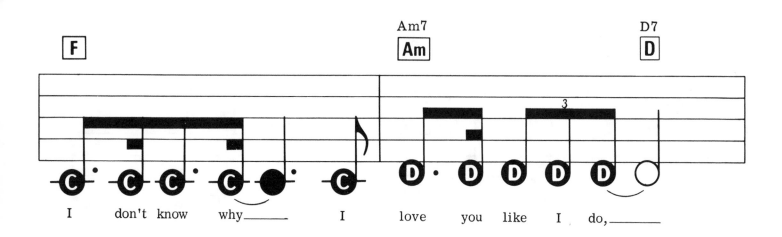

I don't know why____ I love you like I do,____

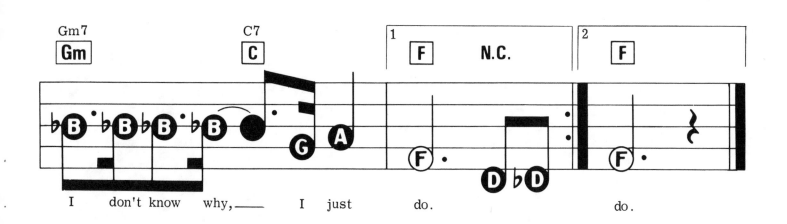

I don't know why,____ I just do. do.

I'll Never Smile Again

Registration 4
Rhythm: Fox Trot or Swing

Words and Music by
Ruth Lowe

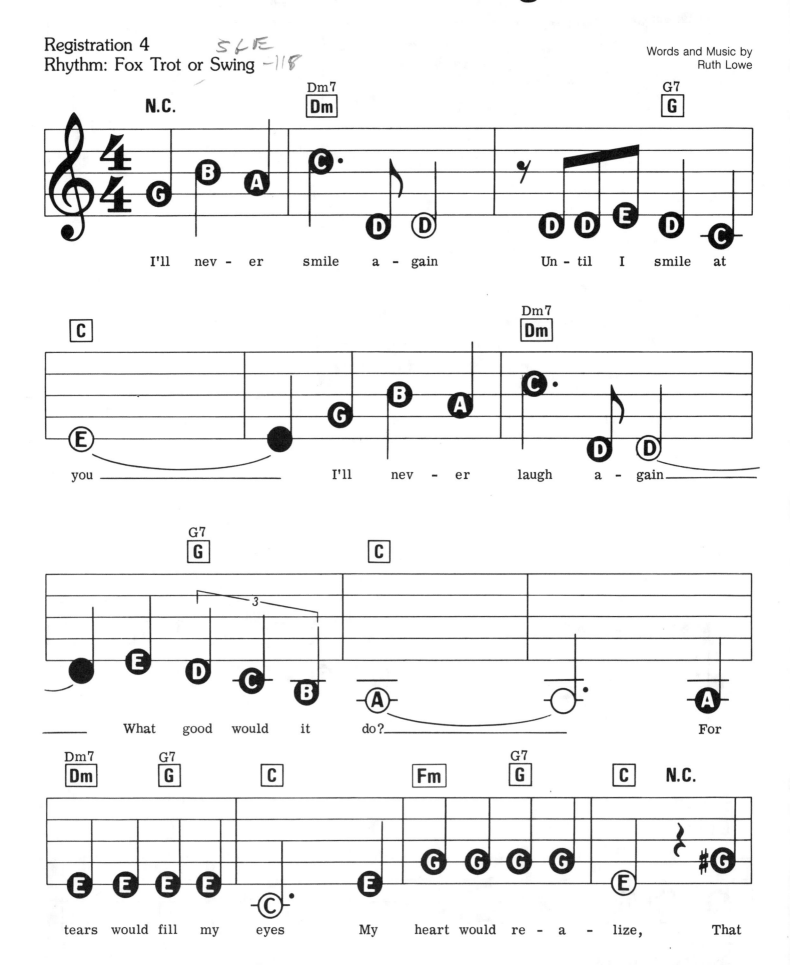

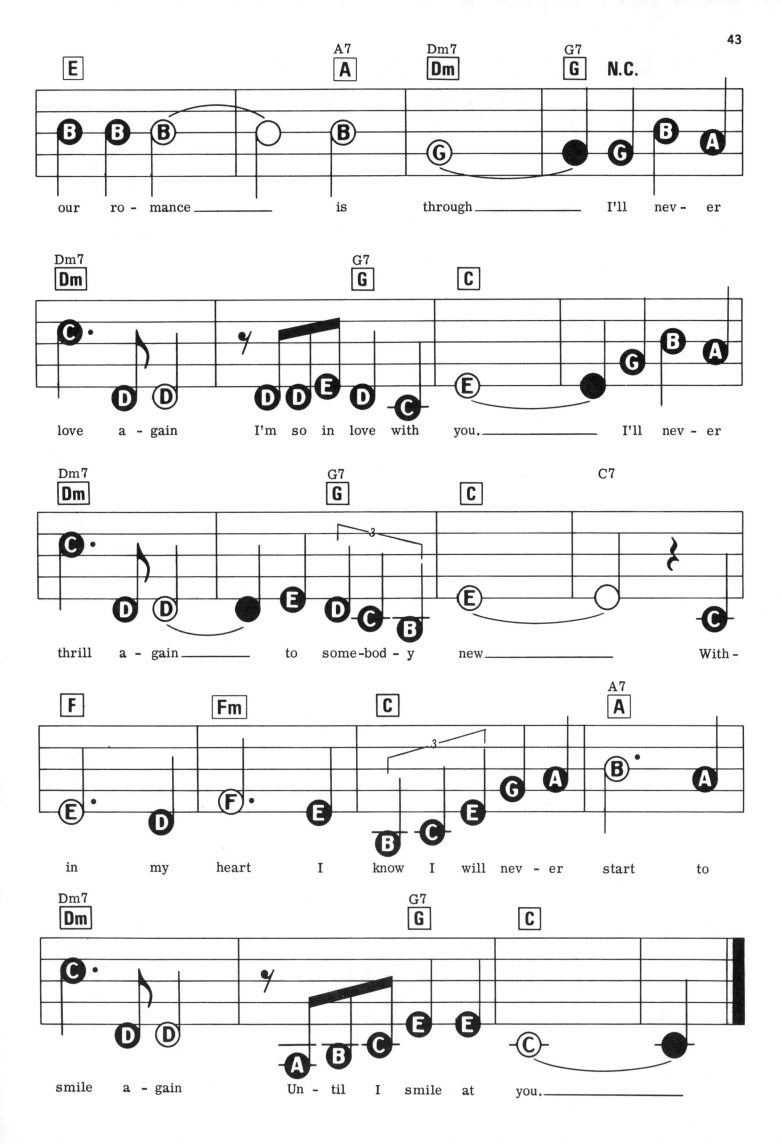

I'm Gonna Sit Right Down And Write Myself A Letter

Registration 3
Rhythm: Fox Trot or Swing ~120

Words by Joe Young
Music by Fred E. Ahlert

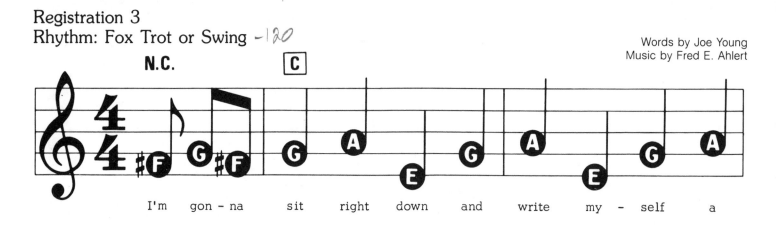

I'm gon - na sit right down and write my - self a

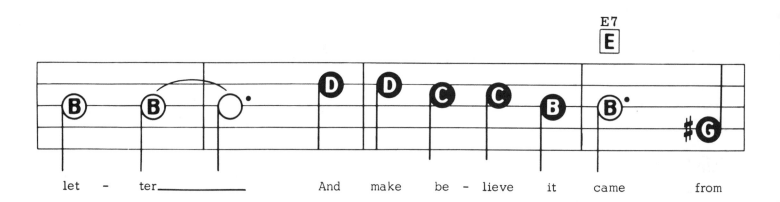

let - ter_____ And make be - lieve it came from

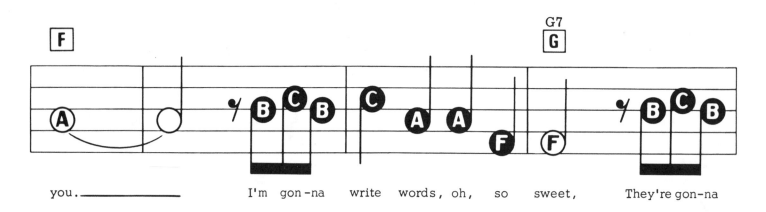

you._____ I'm gon -na write words, oh, so sweet, They're gon-na

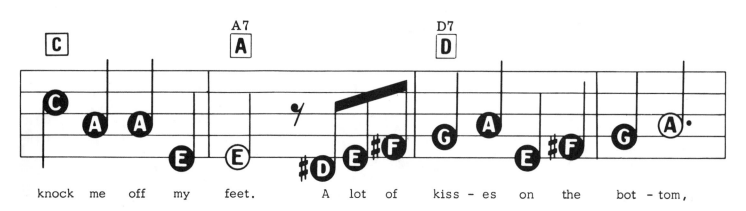

knock me off my feet. A lot of kiss - es on the bot - tom,

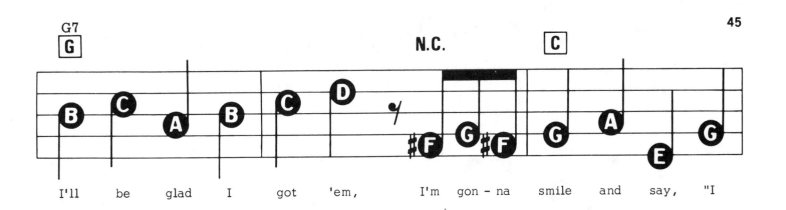

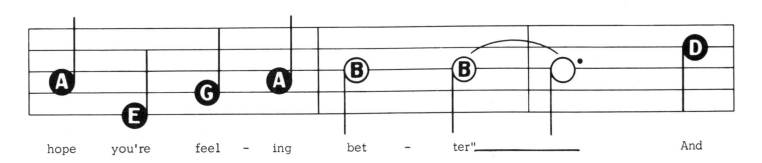

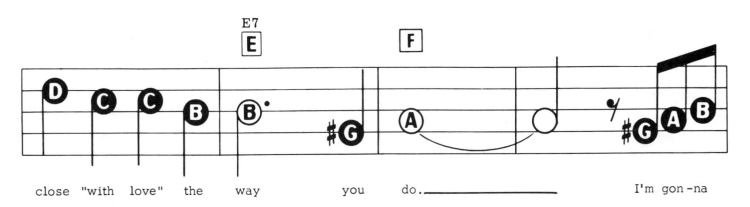

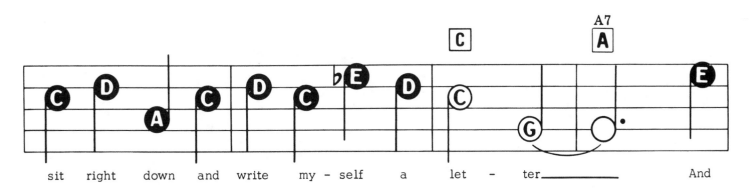

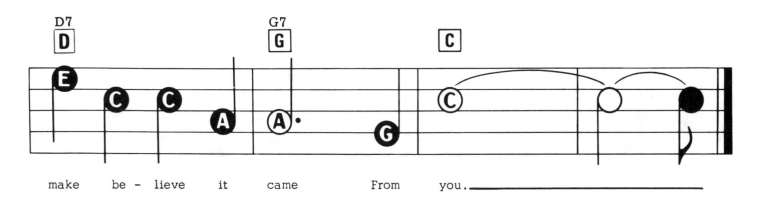

I've Got The World On A String

Registration 1
Rhythm: Swing

Words by Ted Koehler
Music by Harold Arlen

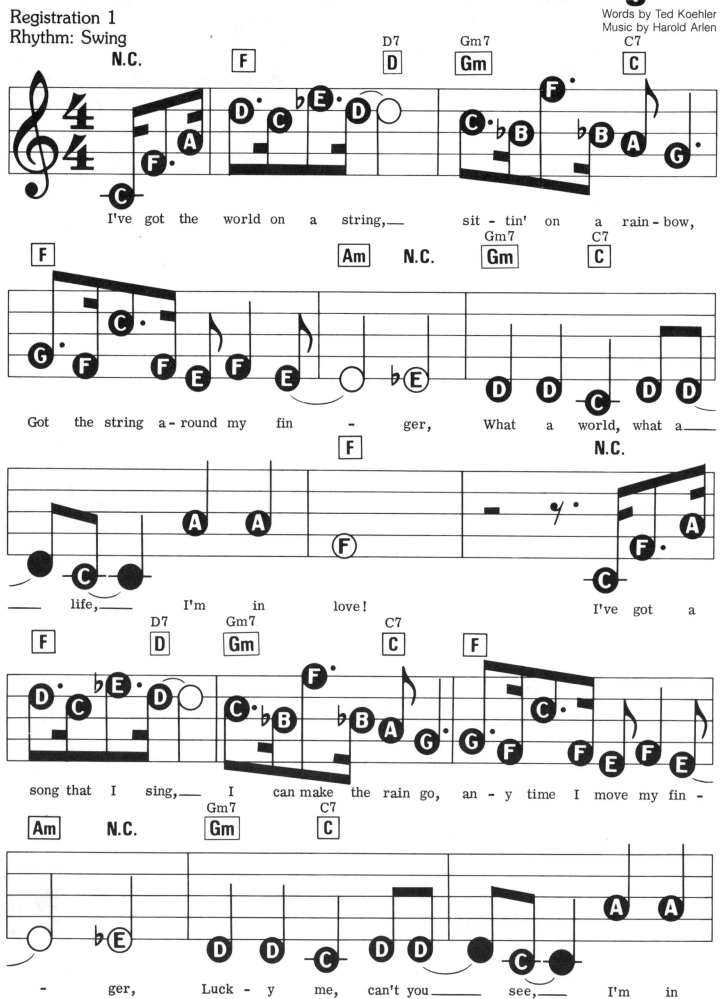

47

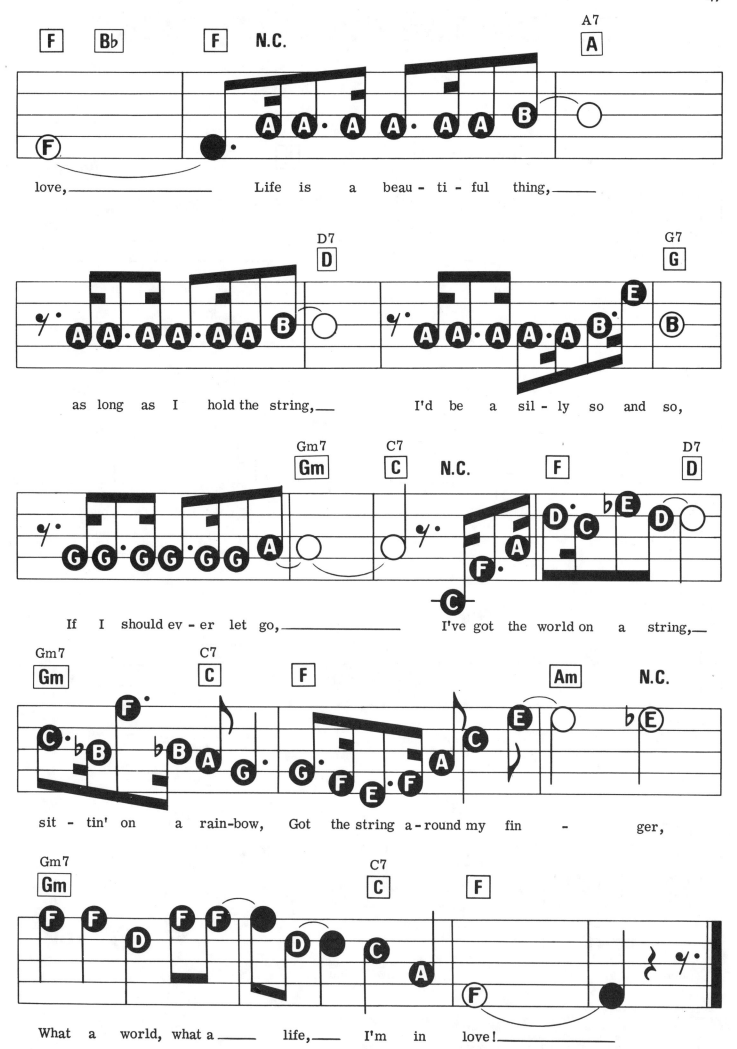

I've Got You Under My Skin

Registration 5
Rhythm: Ballad or Fox Trot —116

Words and Music by
Cole Porter

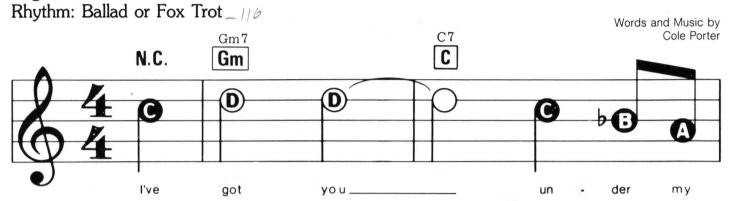

I've got you _____ un - der my

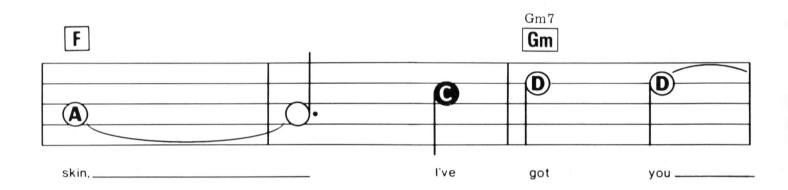

skin, _____ I've got you _____

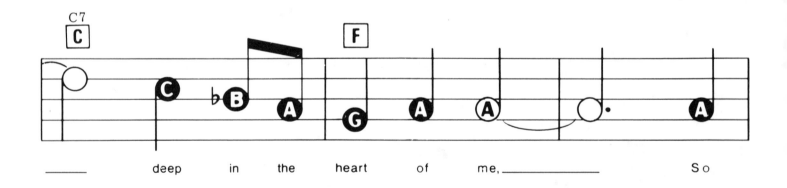

_____ deep in the heart of me, _____ So

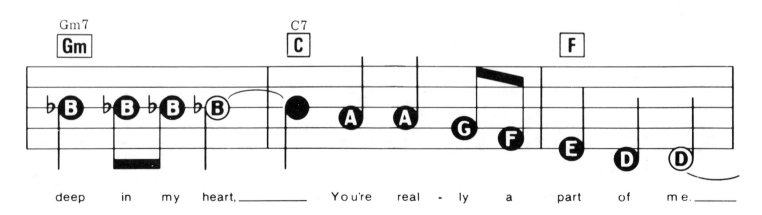

deep in my heart, _____ You're real - ly a part of me. _____

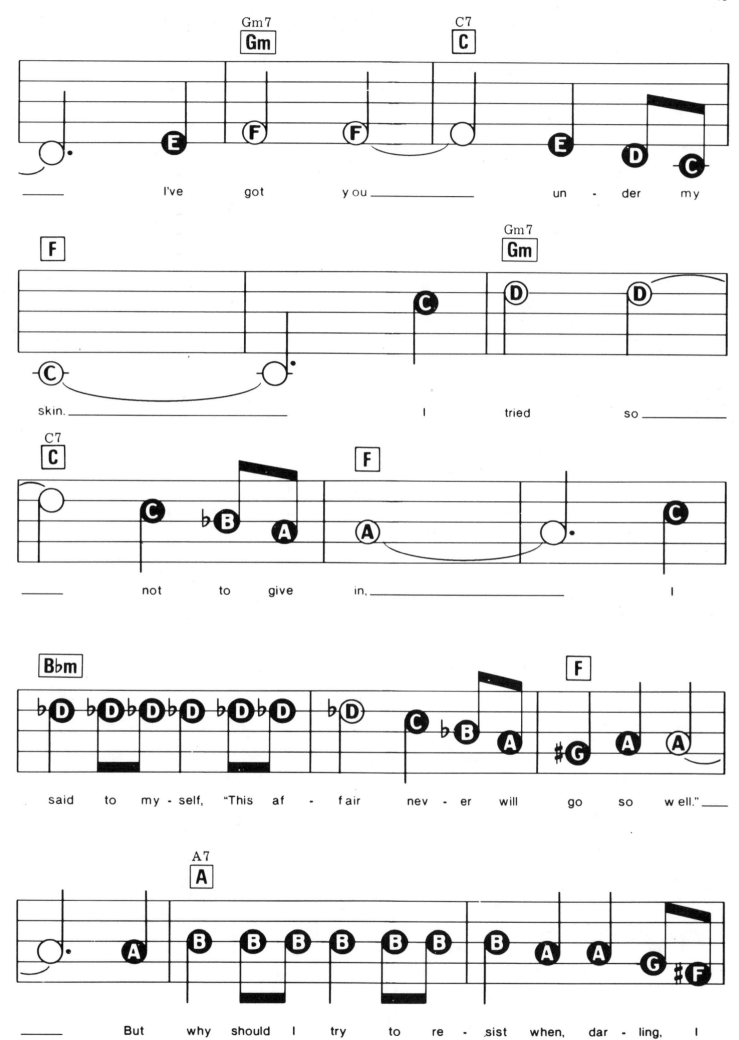

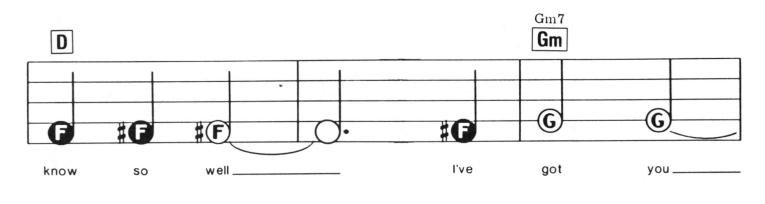

know   so   well _____   I've   got   you _____

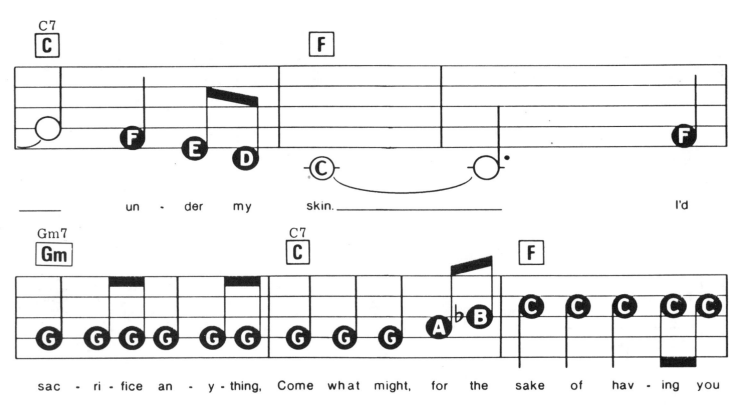

_____   un - der   my   skin. _____   I'd

sac - ri - fice an - y - thing,   Come what might,   for   the   sake   of   hav - ing   you

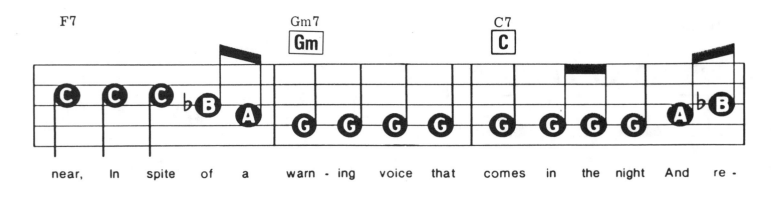

near,   In   spite   of   a   warn - ing   voice   that   comes   in   the   night   And   re -

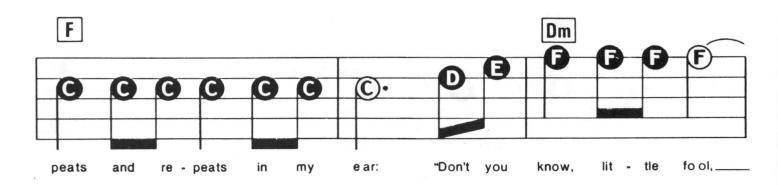

peats   and   re - peats   in   my   ear: "Don't   you   know,   lit - tle   fool, _____

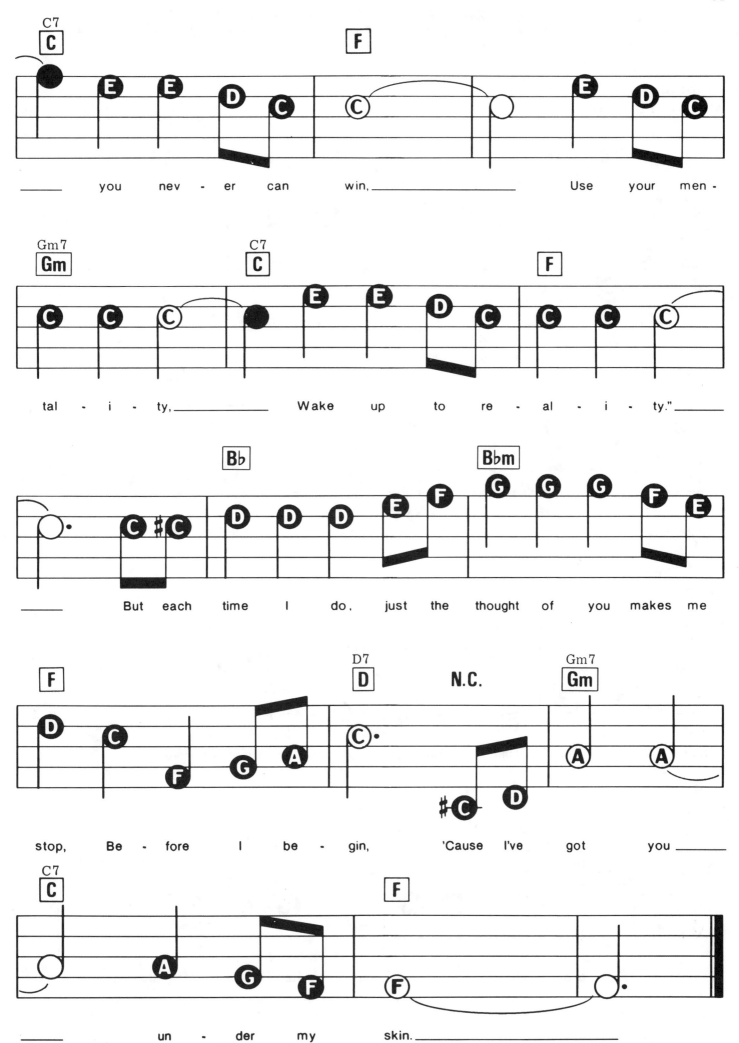

In A Shanty In Old Shanty Town

Registration 2
Rhythm: Fox Trot 130

Words by Joe Young
Music by Little Jack Little and John Siras

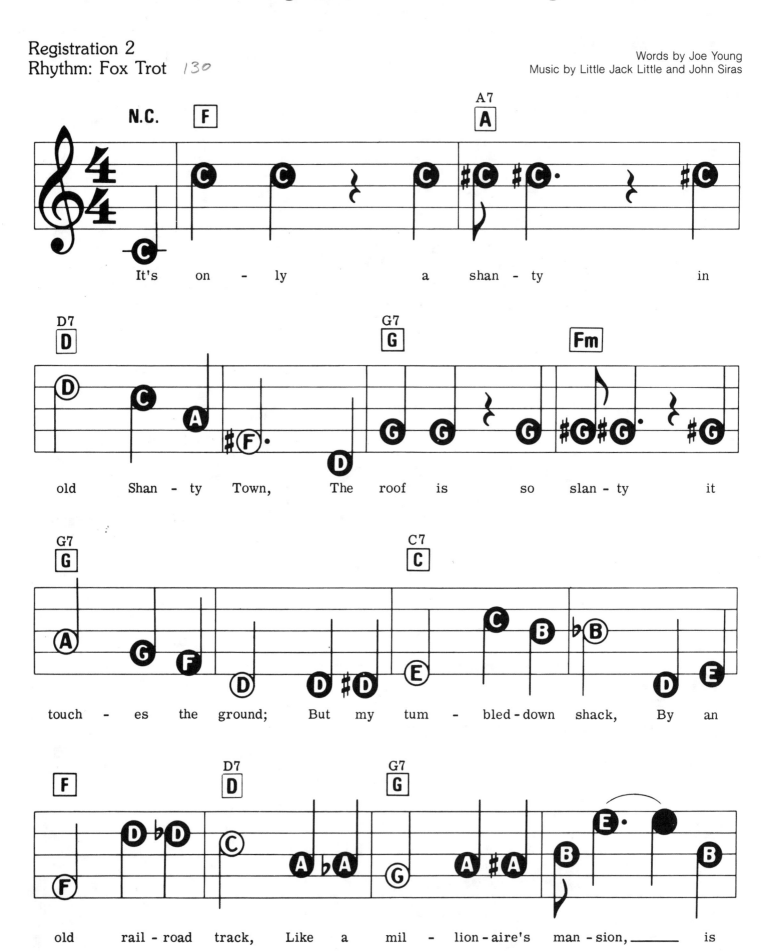

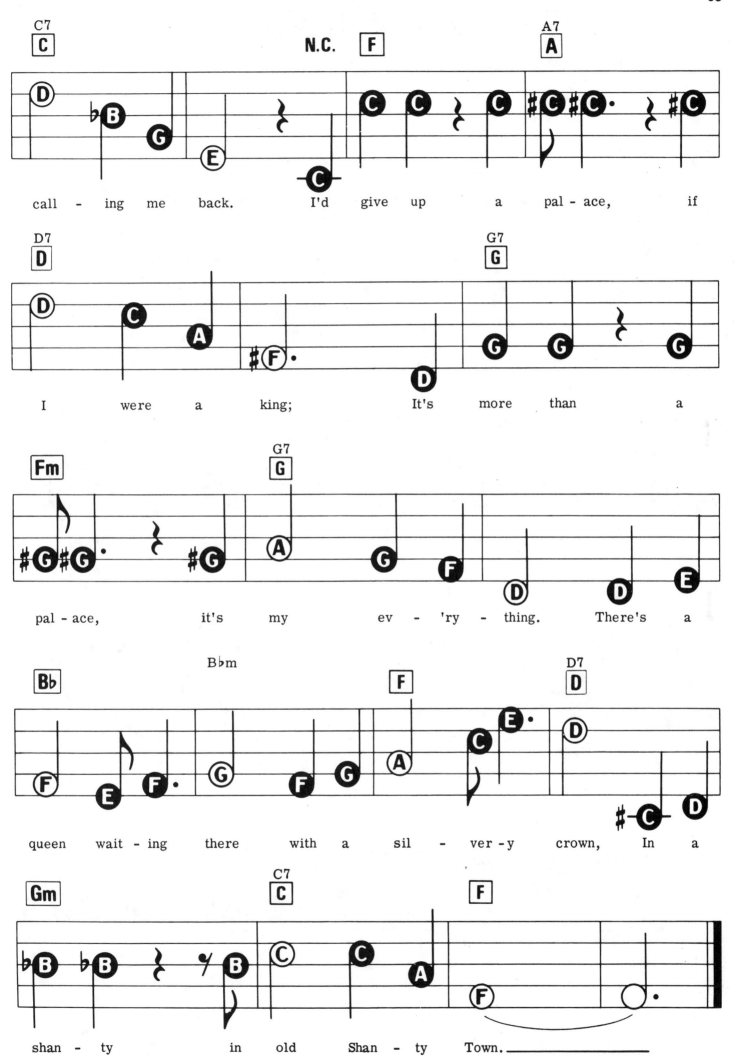

In The Mood

Registration 8
Rhythm: Fox Trot or Swing ~120

Words and Music by
Joe Garland

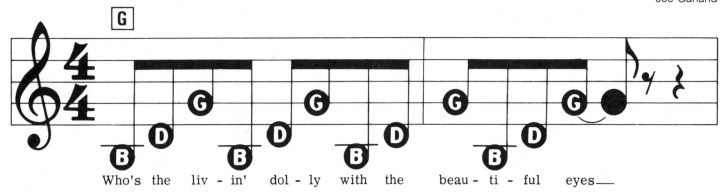

Who's the liv - in' dol - ly with the beau - ti - ful eyes___

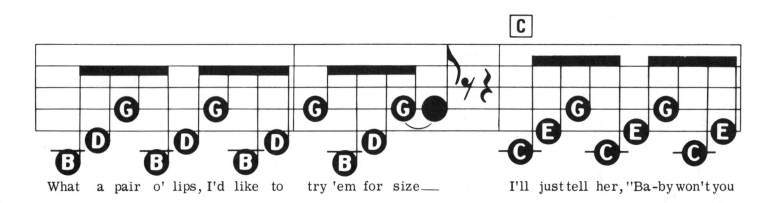

What a pair o' lips, I'd like to try 'em for size___ I'll just tell her, "Ba-by won't you

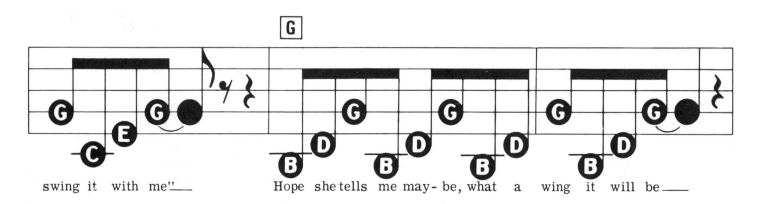

swing it with me"___ Hope she tells me may- be, what a wing it will be___

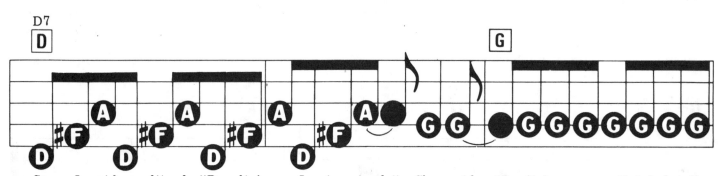

So, I said po - lite-ly, "Dar-lin' may I in - trude"___ She said___ "Don't keep me wait-in' when I'm

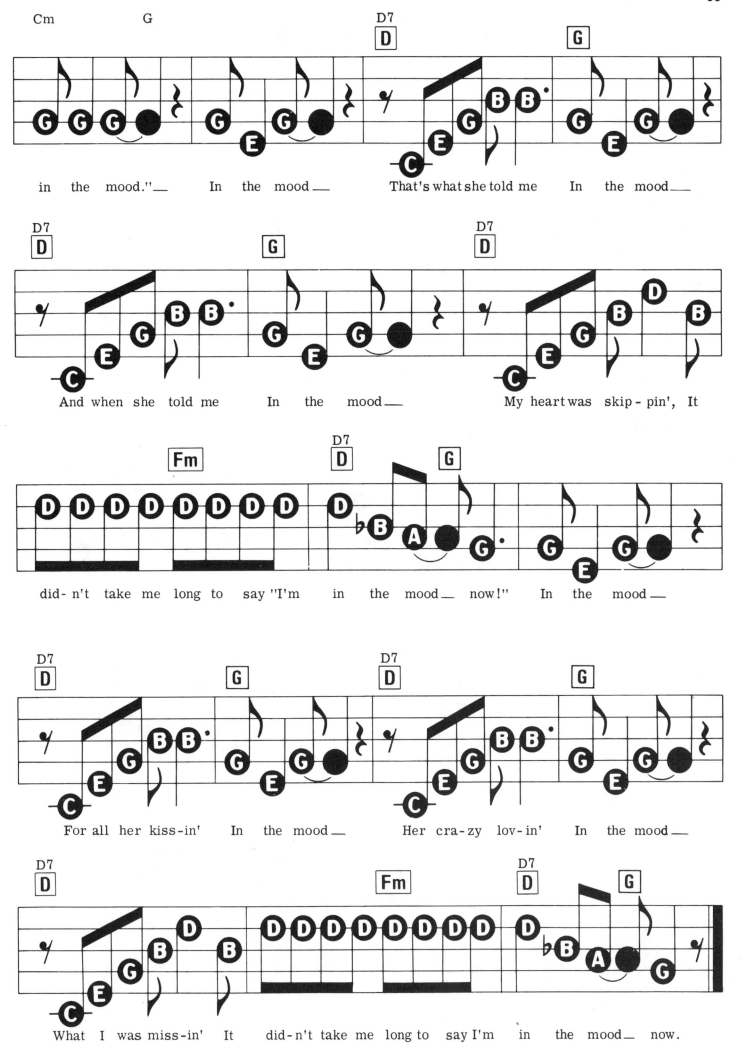

In The Still Of The Night

Registration 2
Rhythm: Latin

Words and Music by
Cole Porter

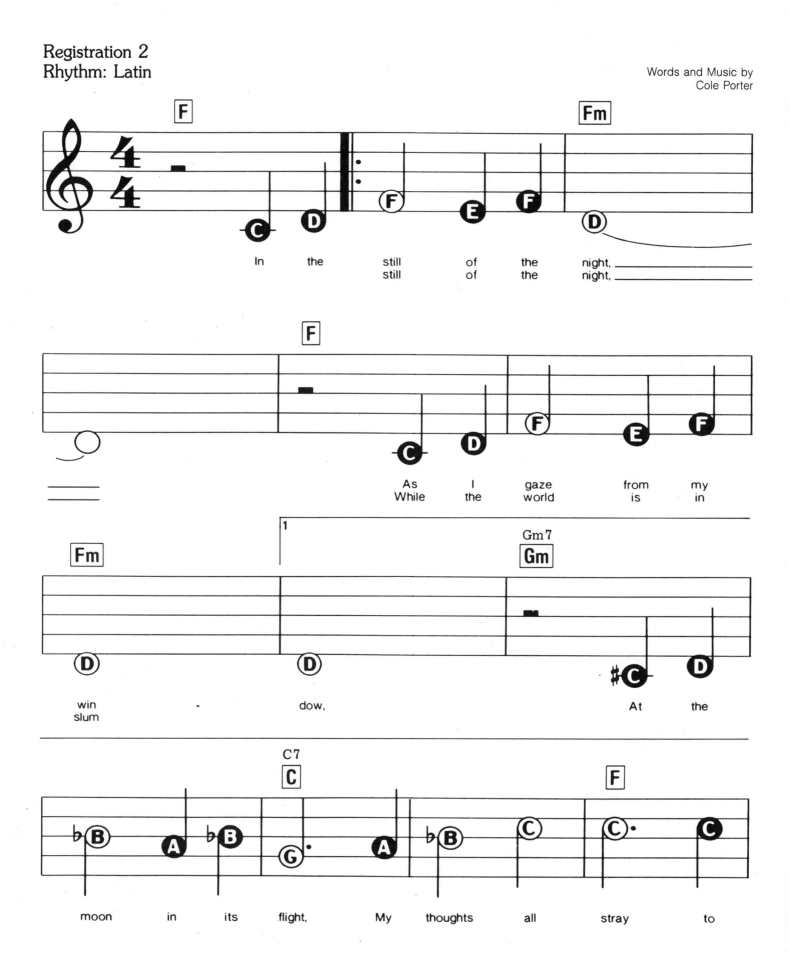

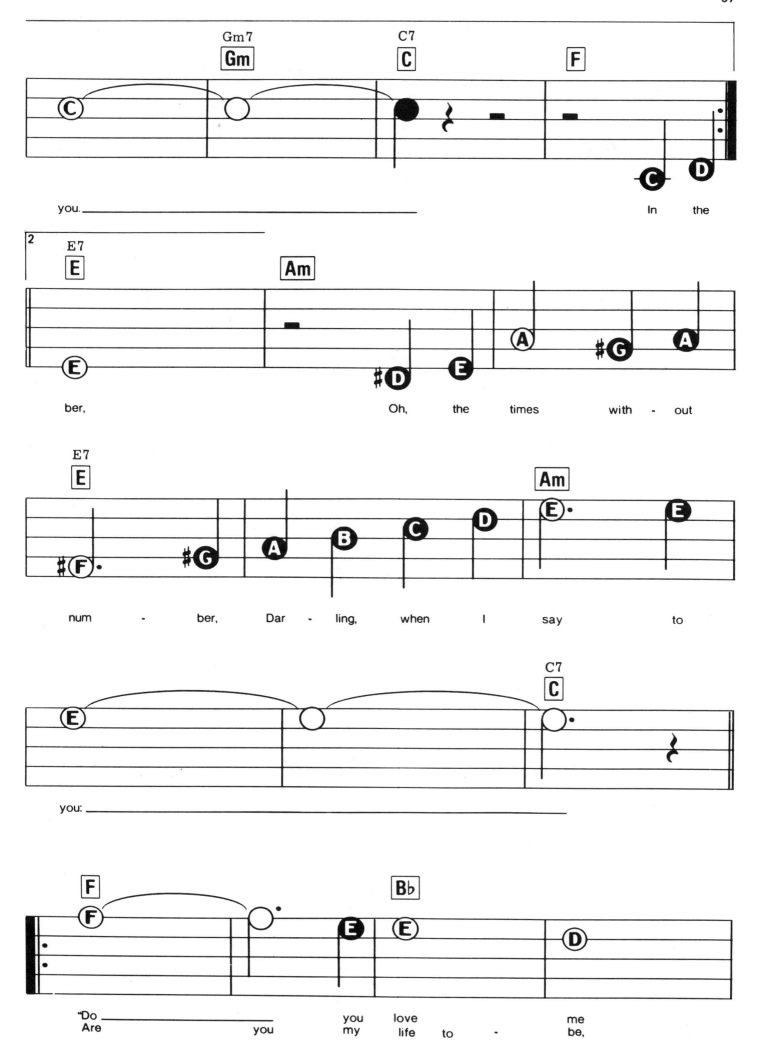

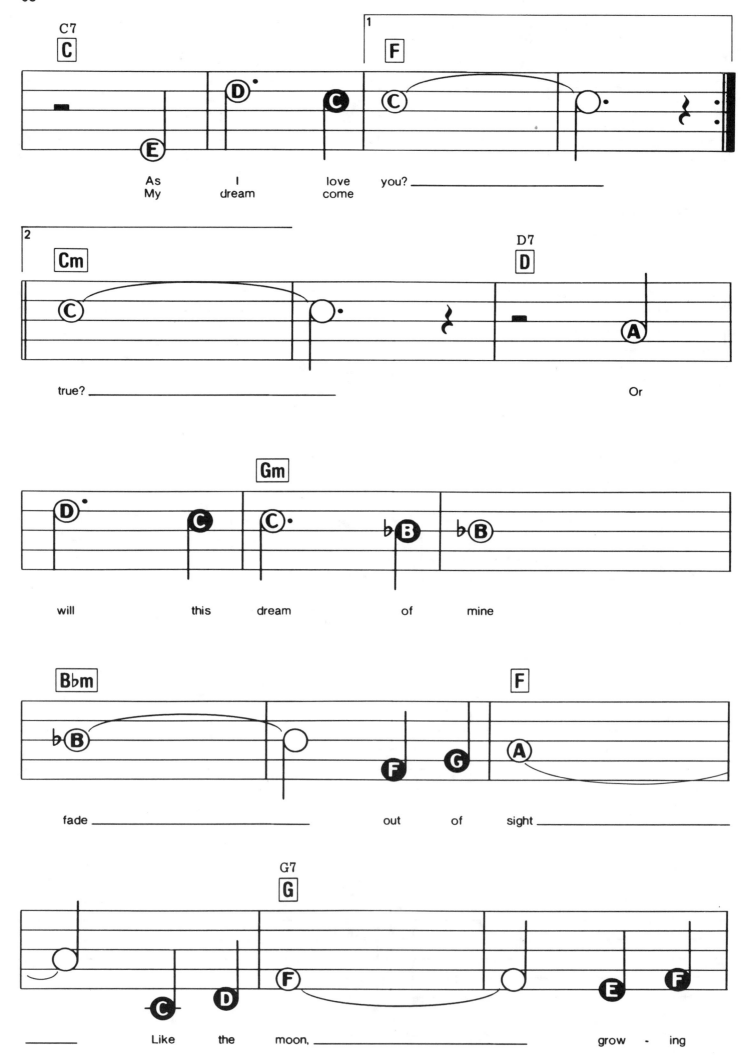

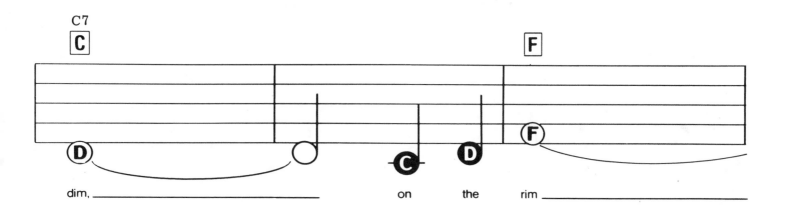

dim, _____ on the rim _____

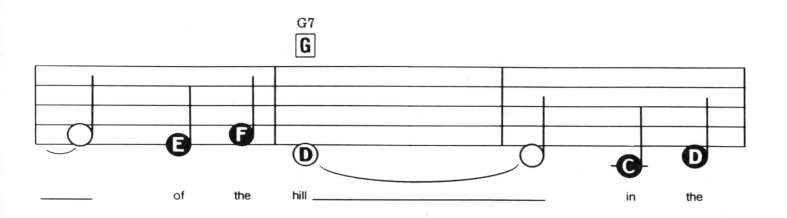

_____ of the hill _____ in the

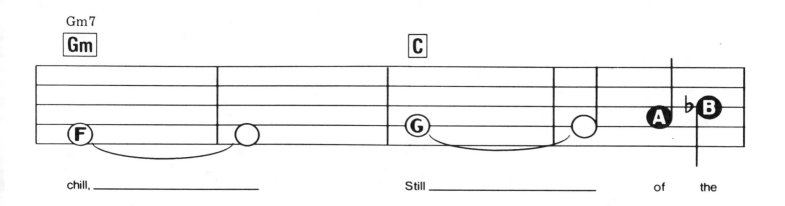

chill, _____ Still _____ of the

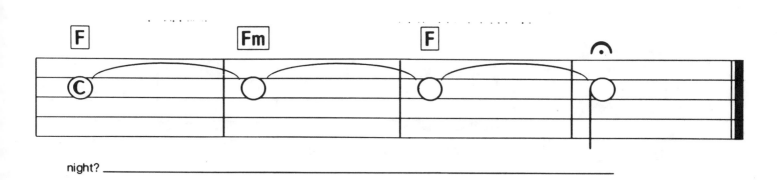

night? _____

It Ain't Necessarily So

Words by Ira Gershwin
Music by George Gershwin

Registration 7
Rhythm: Ballad

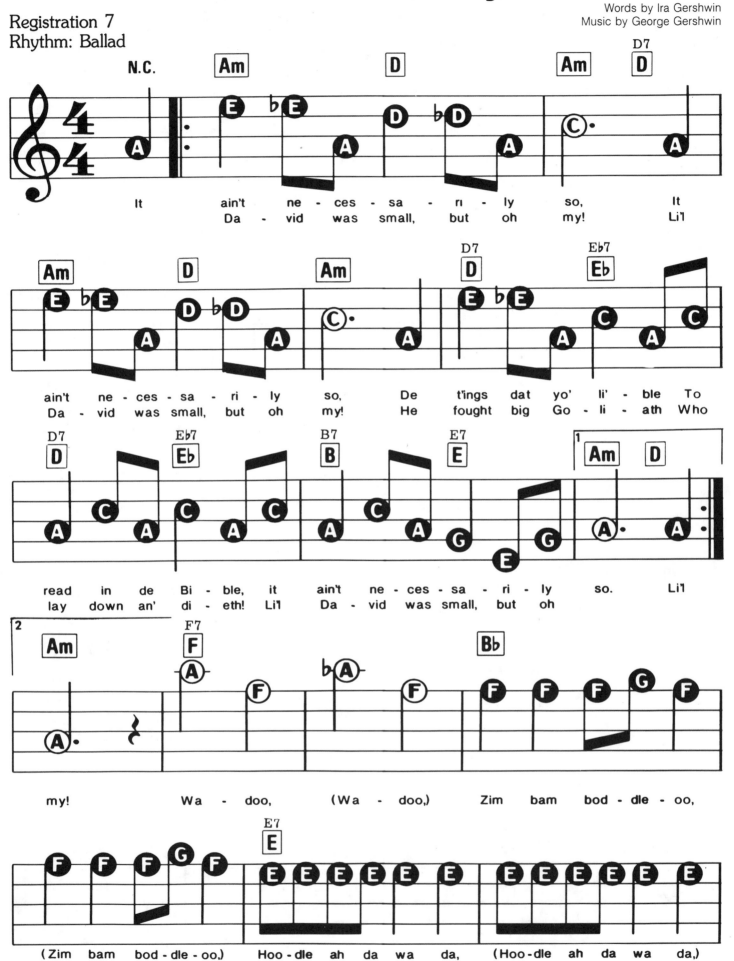

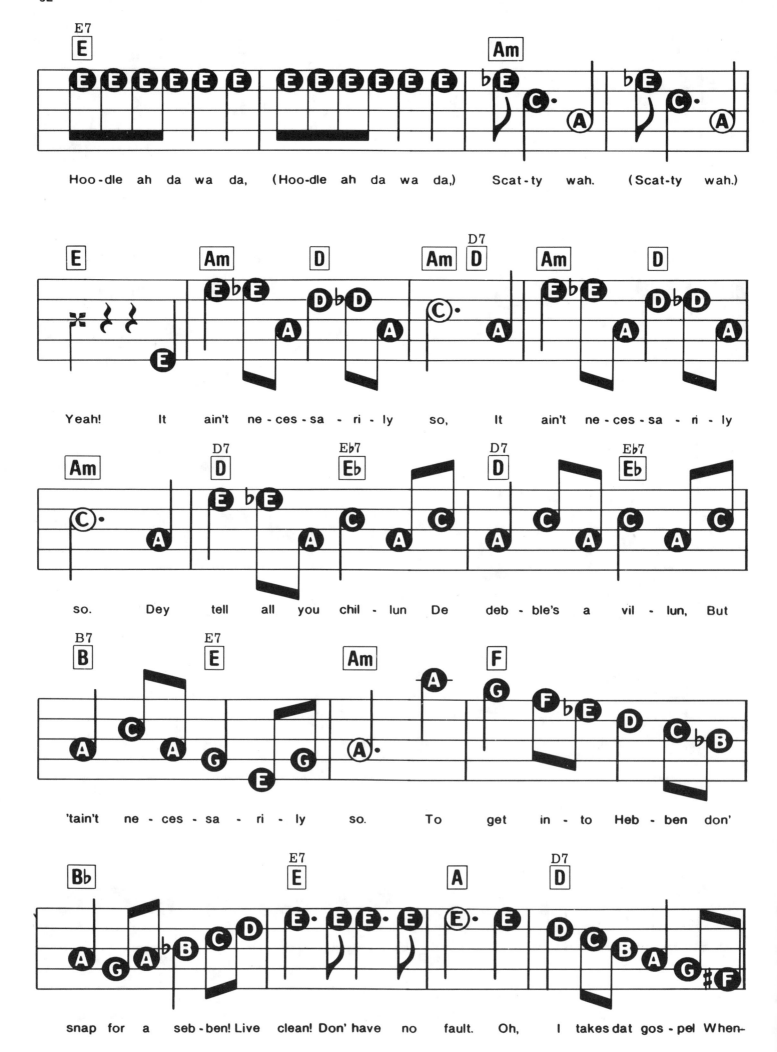

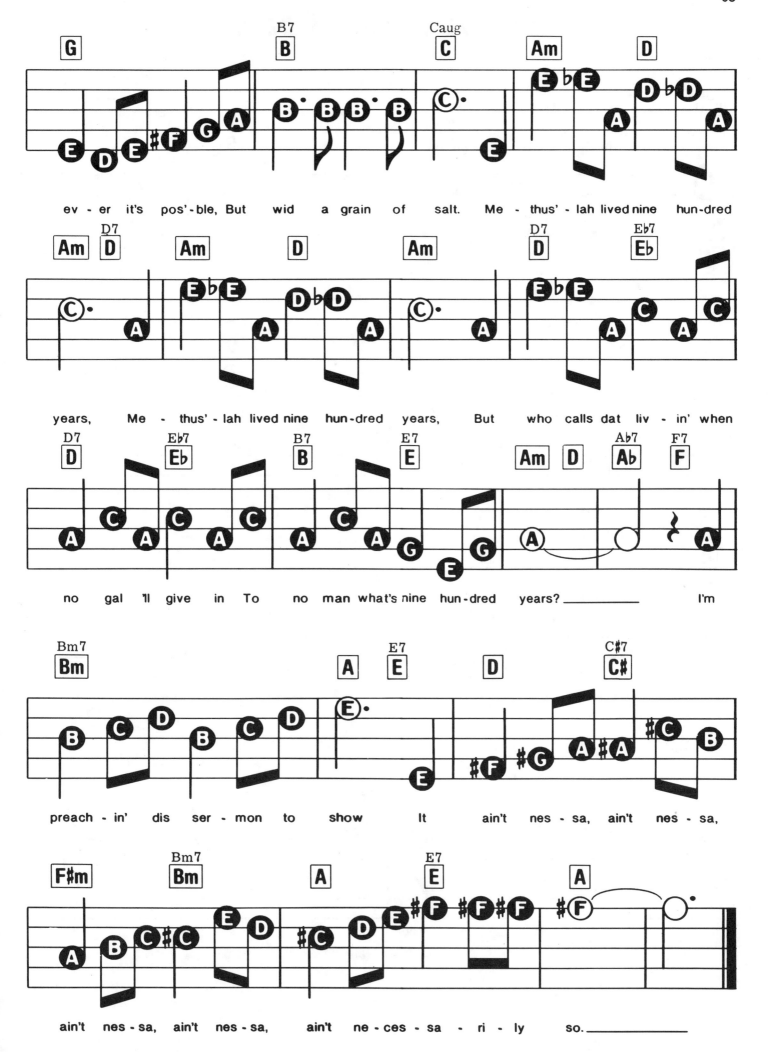

It's A Blue World

Registration 2
Rhythm: Fox Trot

Words and Music by
Bob Wright and Chet Forrest

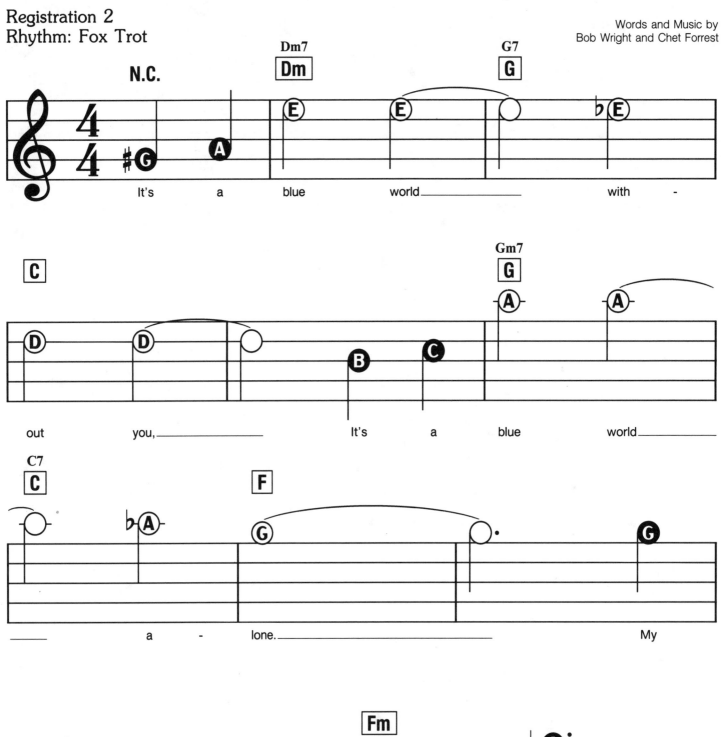

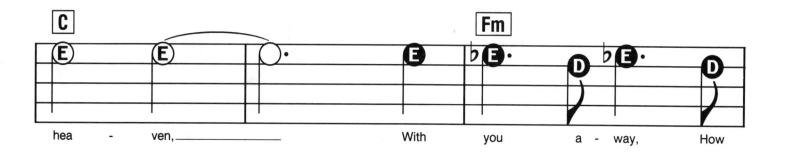

hea - ven,_____ With you a - way, How

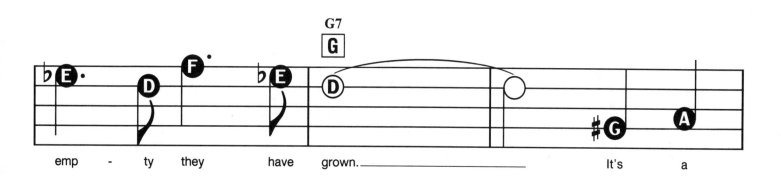

emp - ty they have grown._____ It's a

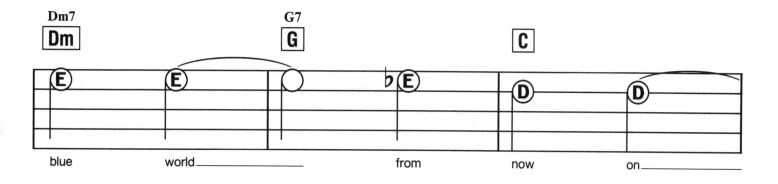

blue world_____ from now on_____

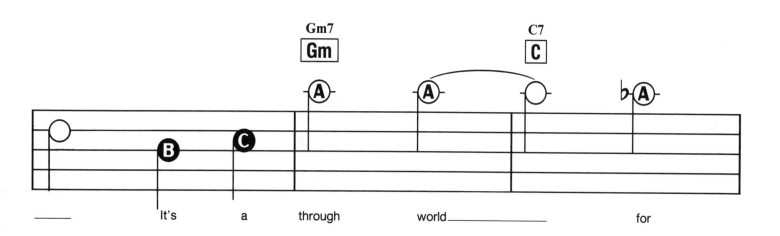

_____ It's a through world_____ for

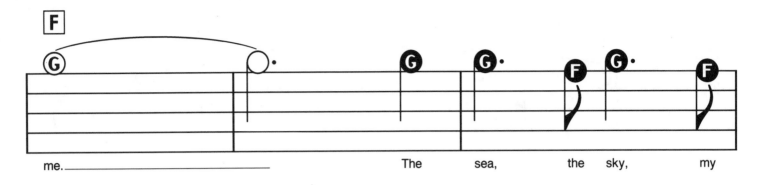

me._____ The sea, the sky, my

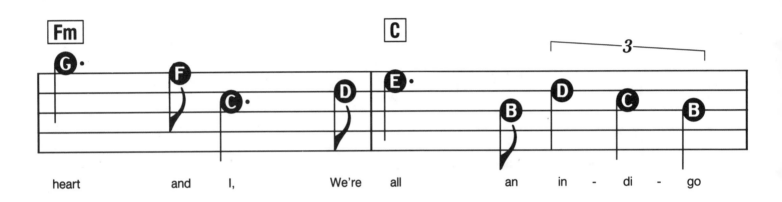

heart and I, We're all an in - di - go

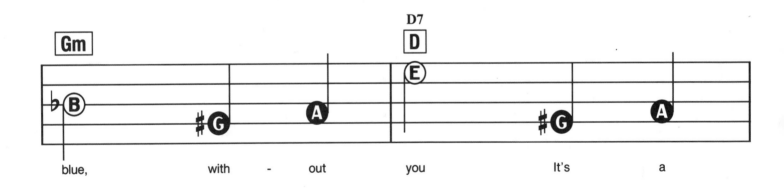

blue, with - out you It's a

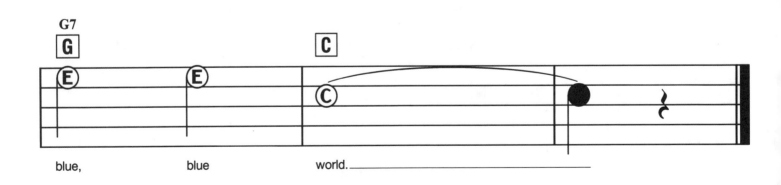

blue, blue world._____

Say "Si, Si"

Registration 3
Rhythm: Fox Trot or Swing

Music by Ernesto Lecuona
Spanish Words by Francia Luban
English Words by Al Stillman

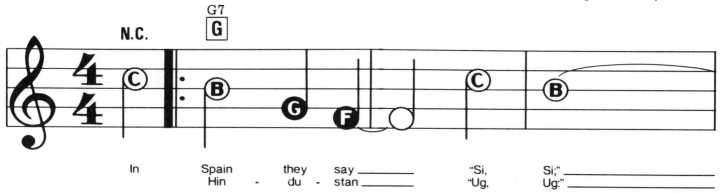

In Spain they say _____ "Si, Si;" _____
Hin - du - stan _____ "Ug, Ug:" _____

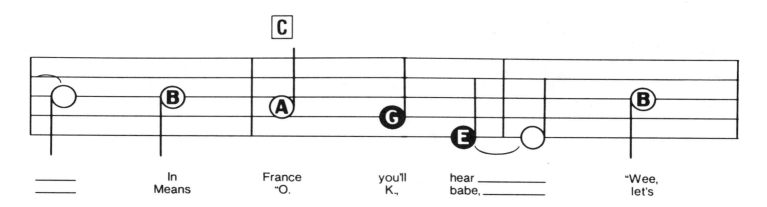

_____ In France you'll hear _____ "Wee,
_____ Means "O. K., babe, _____ let's

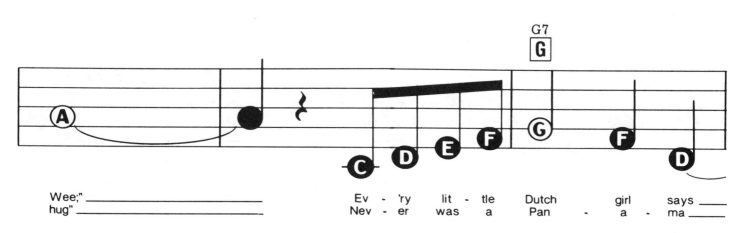

Wee;" _____ Ev - 'ry lit - tle Dutch girl says _____
hug" _____ Nev - er was a Dutch Pan - a - ma _____

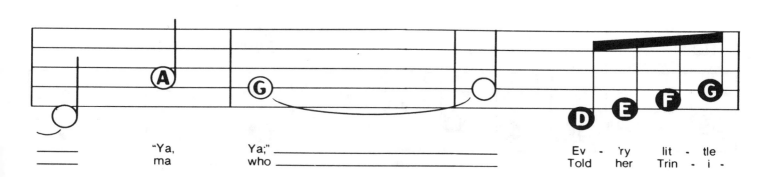

_____ "Ya, Ya;" _____ Ev - 'ry lit - tle
_____ ma who _____ Told her Trin - i -

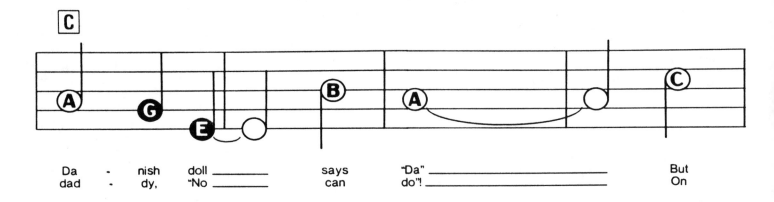

Da - nish doll _____ says "Da" _____ But
dad - dy, "No _____ can do"! _____ On

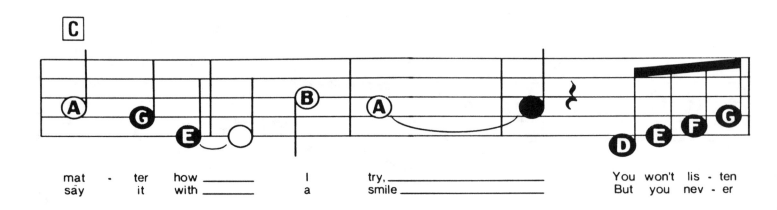

sweet - heart tell _____ me why, _____ No
ev - 'ry Vir - gin Isle _____ They

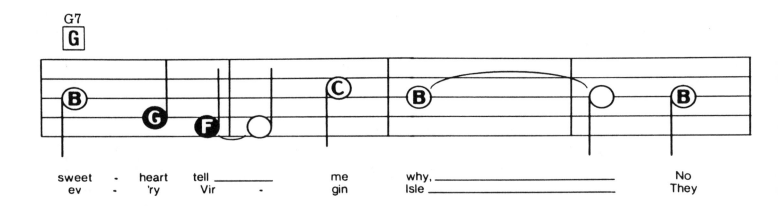

mat - ter how _____ I try, _____ You won't lis - ten
say it with _____ a smile _____ But you nev - er

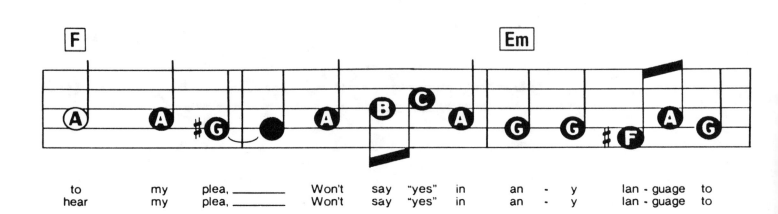

to my plea, _____ Won't say "yes" in an - y lan - guage to
hear my plea, _____ Won't say "yes" in an - y lan - guage to

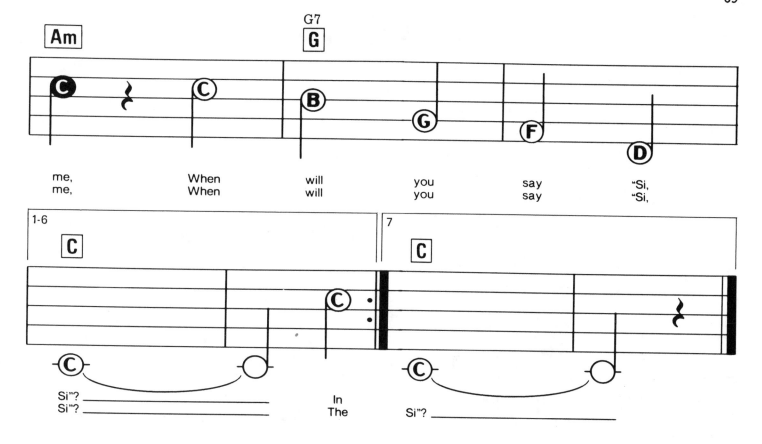

me, When will you say "Si,
me, When will you say "Si,

Si"?
Si"?

In
The Si"?

3rd Chorus

The monkeys in the tree
Don't have to say: "Si, Si",
All they do is wag their little tails;
That's a little gag that never fails.
In darkest Africa
The natives say: "Uh, Huh!"
But you never hear my plea,
Won't say "Yes" in any language to me
When will you say: "Si, Si"?

5th Chorus

In Washington, D.C.,
The yes-men say: "Si, Si";
There are lots of politicians, though
Who can always say both "Yes" and "No".
But sweetheart tell me why,
No matter how I try,
you won't listen to my plea
Won't say "Yes" in any language to me
When will you say "Si, Si"?

4th Chorus

Out West they say: "Wah Hoo!"
That's "O.K., Toots" to you.
Every Southern lady knows her stuff,
'Cause her answer is "Sho Nuff!"
But, sweetheart, tell me why,
No matter how I try.
You won't listen to my plea,
Won't say "Yes" in any language to me
When will you say: "Si, Si"?

6th Chorus

A lady horse, they say,
Means "Yes" when she says: "Neigh!"
Every little gal from Mexico
Hates to give a pal a "No, No, No!"
So, sweetheart, tell me why,
No matter how I try,
You won't listen to my plea
Won't say "Yes" in any language to me
When will you say "Si, Si"?

7th Chorus

In 606 B.C.,
Those gals would mix, Si, Si!
Every little cave man used his dome,
Hit 'em on the head, then dragged 'em home.
So, sweetheart, tell me why,
No matter how I try,
You won't listen to my plea
Won't say "Yes" in any language to me,
When will you say: "Si, Si"?

It's De-Lovely

Registration 2
Rhythm: Swing

Words and Music by
Cole Porter

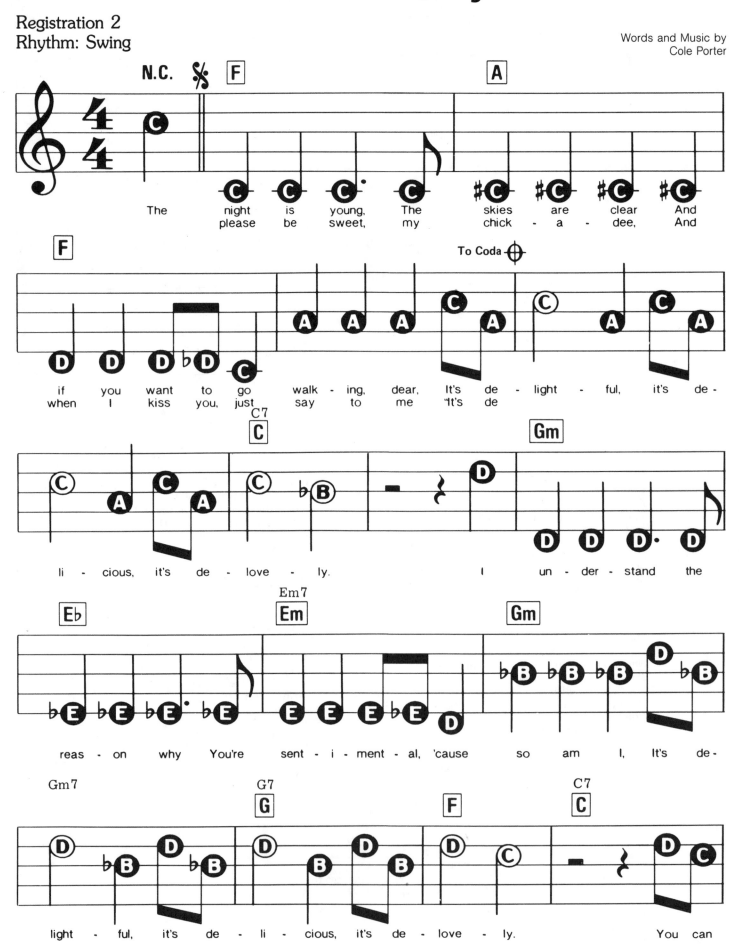

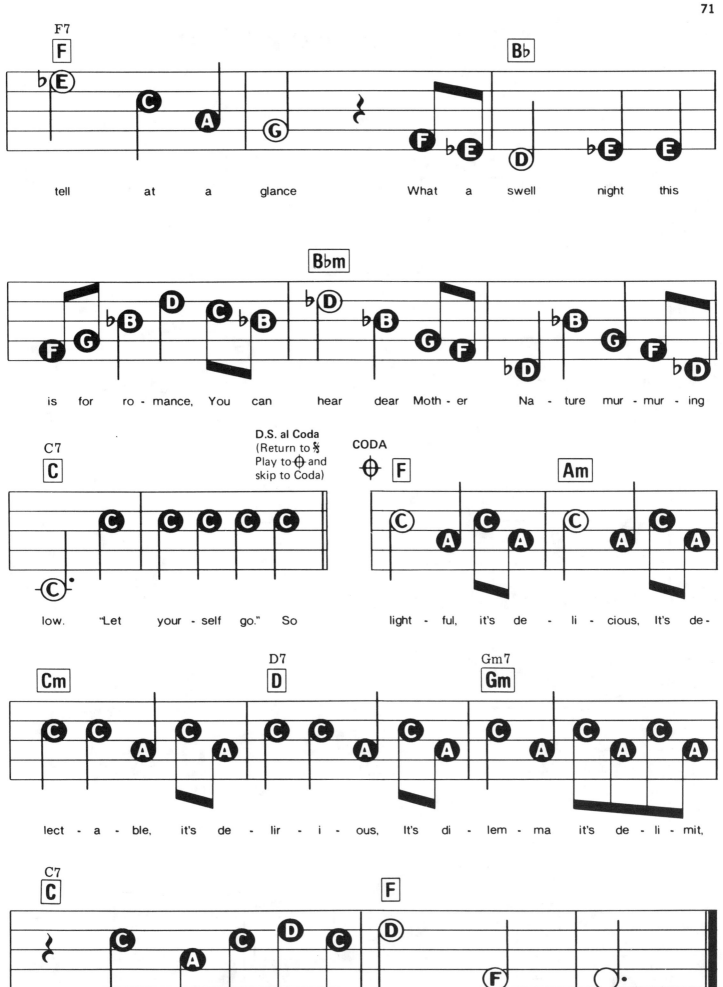

*Pronounced "delukes"

It's Only A Paper Moon

Registration 8
Rhythm: Fox Trot or Swing

Words by Billy Rose & F.Y. Harburg
Music by Harold Arlen

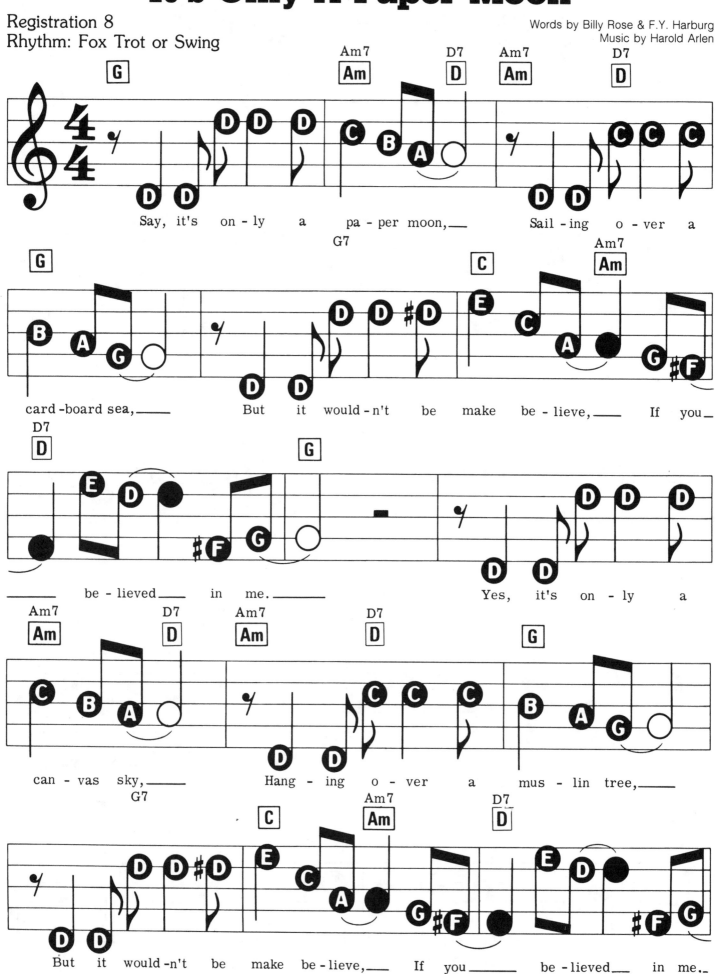

73

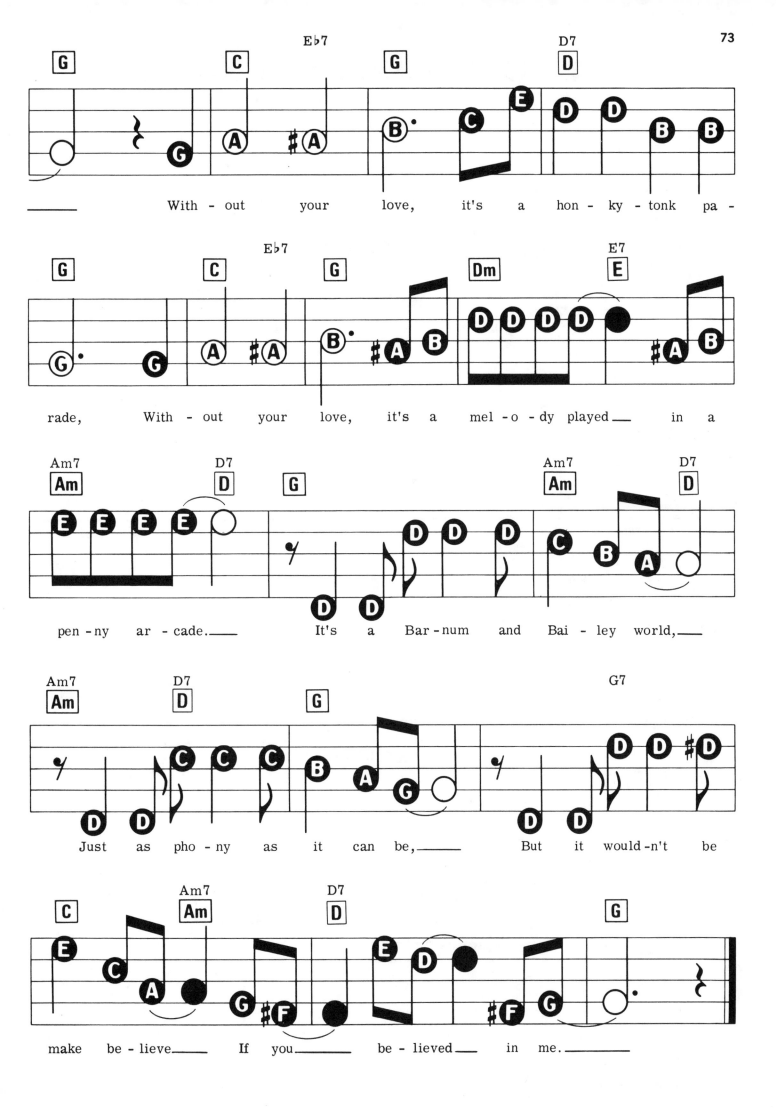

It's The Talk Of The Town

Registration 4
Rhythm: Fox Trot or Swing

Words by Marty Symes and A.J. Neiburg
Music by Jerry Livingston

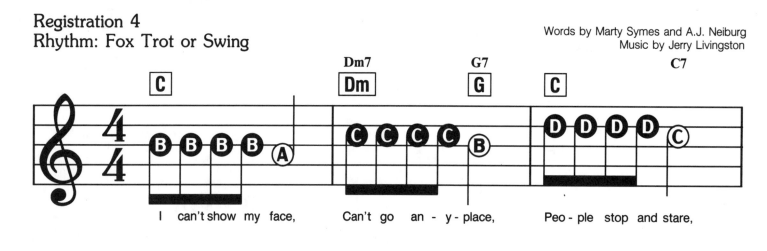

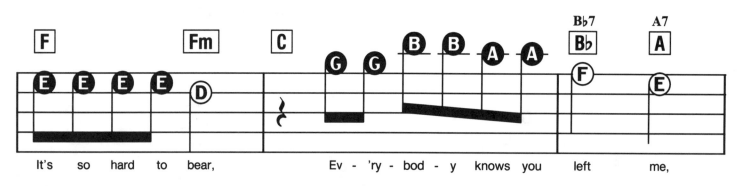

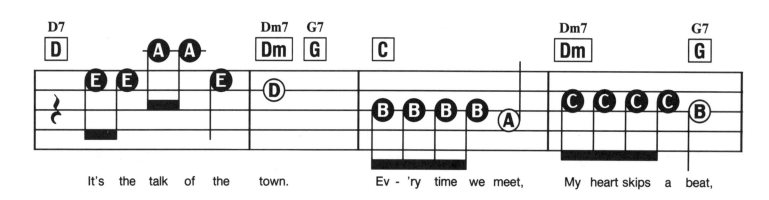

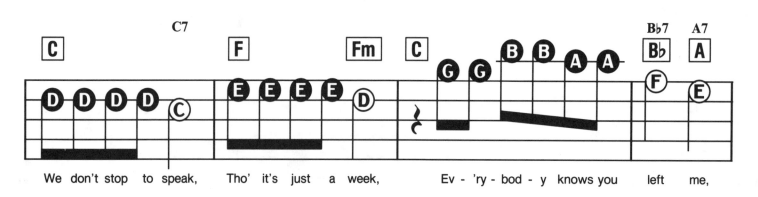

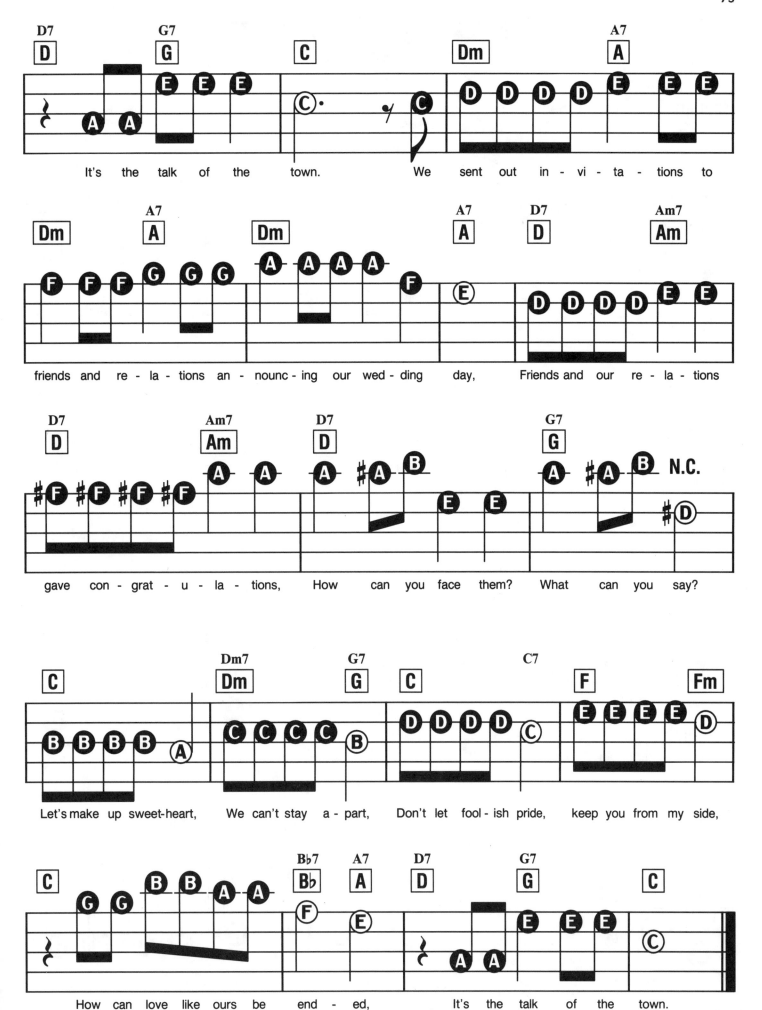

The Lady Is A Tramp

(From "BABES IN ARMS")

Registration 7
Rhythm: Fox Trot or Swing

Words by Lorenz Hart
Music by Richard Rodgers

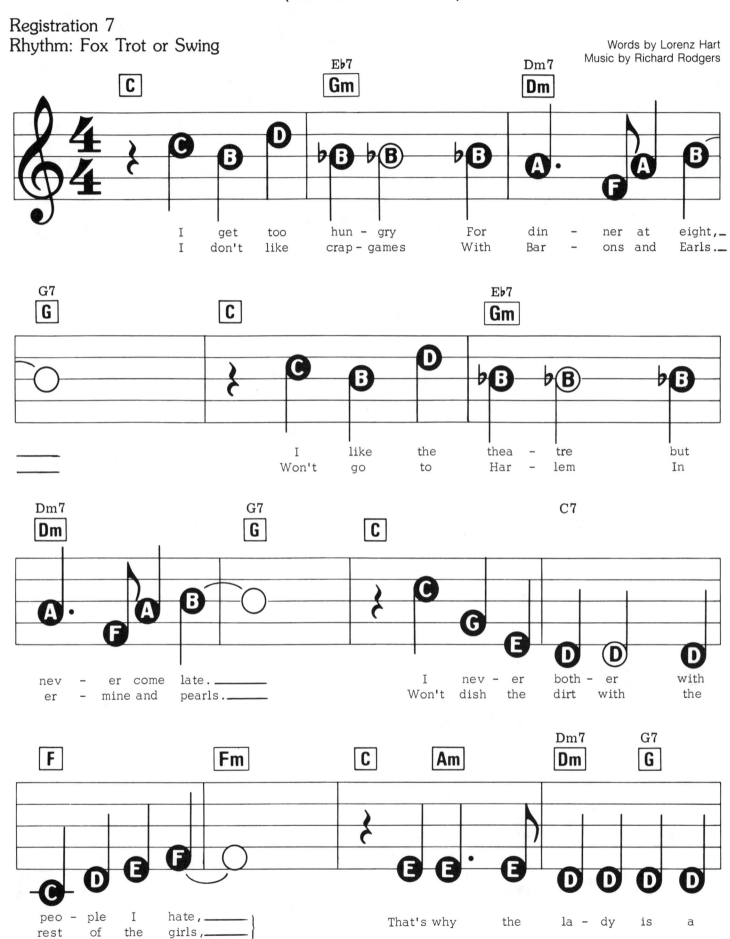

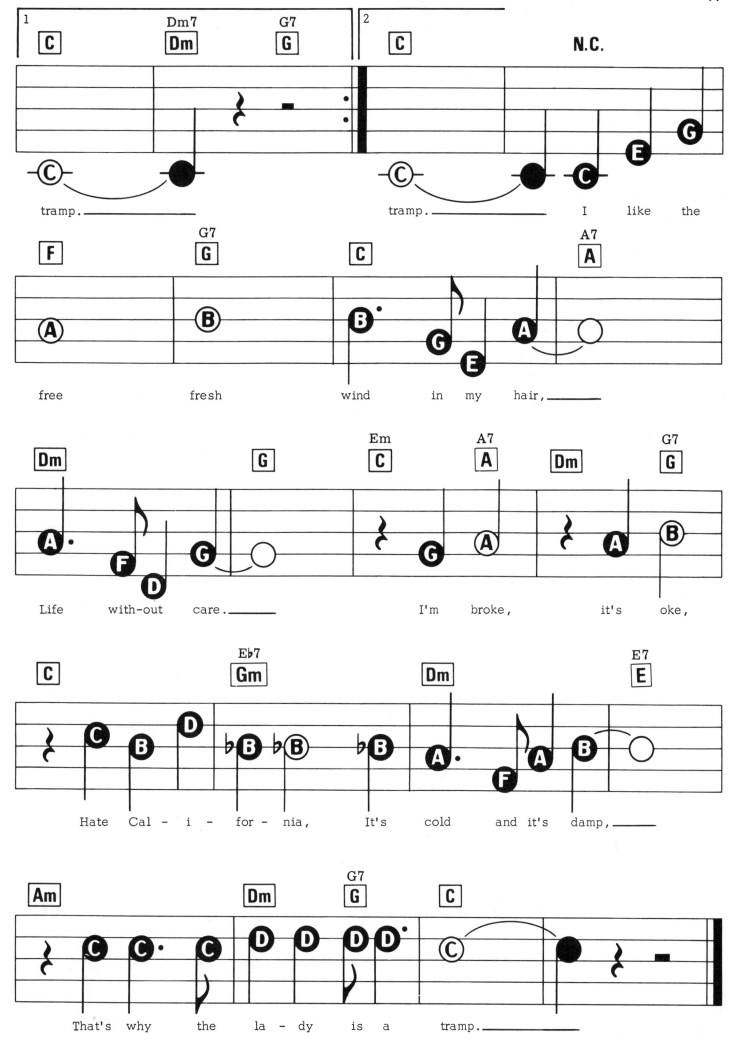

Let's Dance

Registartion 7
Rhythm: Swing or Jazz

Words and Music by Fanny Baldridge,
Gregory Stone and Joseph Bonime

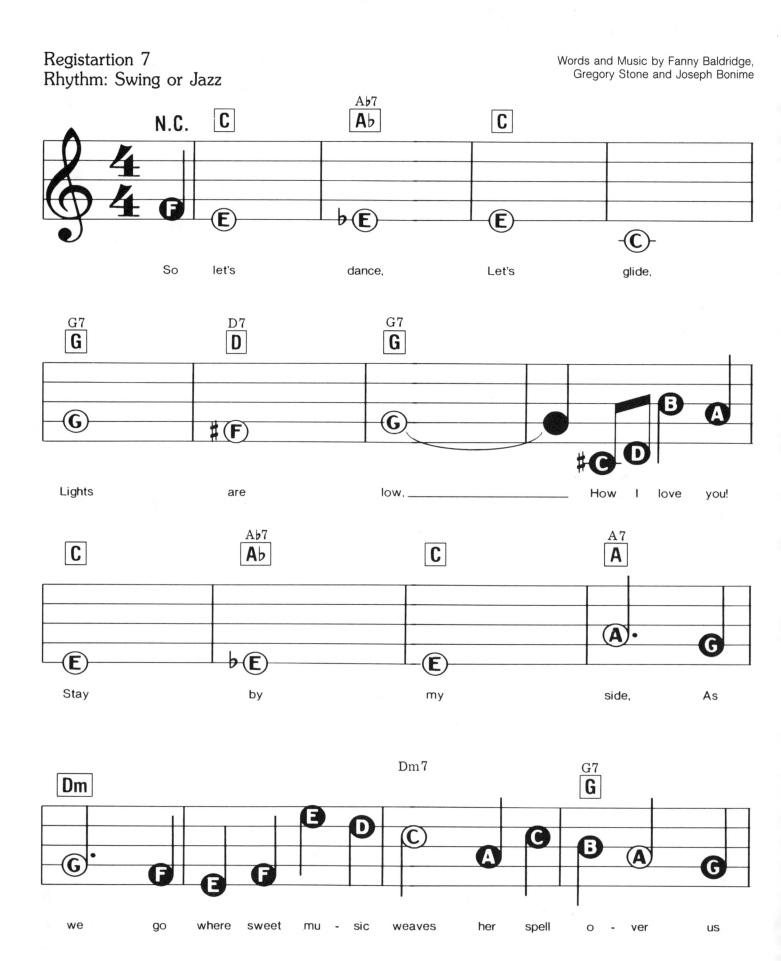

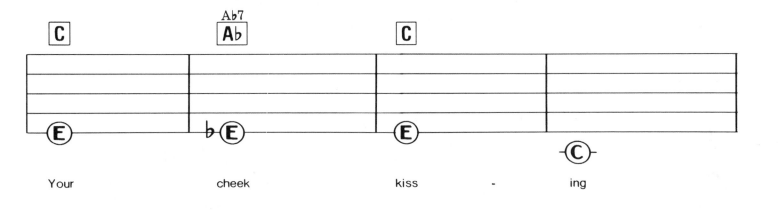

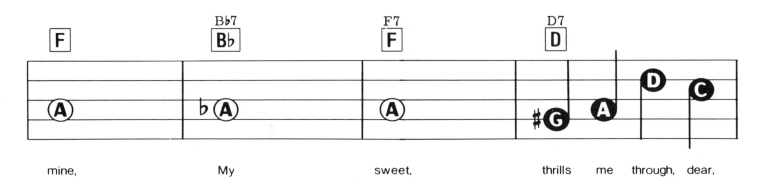

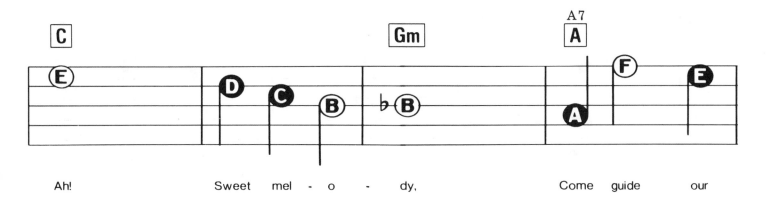

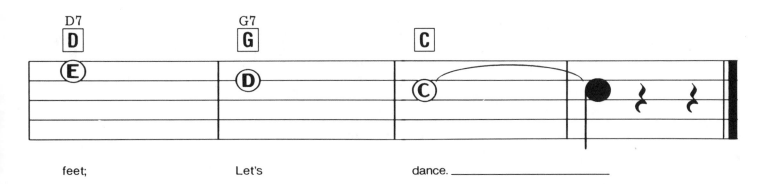

Love Is Here To Stay

(From GOLDWYN FOLLIES)

Registration 4
Rhythm: Fox Trot or Ballad

Words by Ira Gershwin
Music by George Gershwin

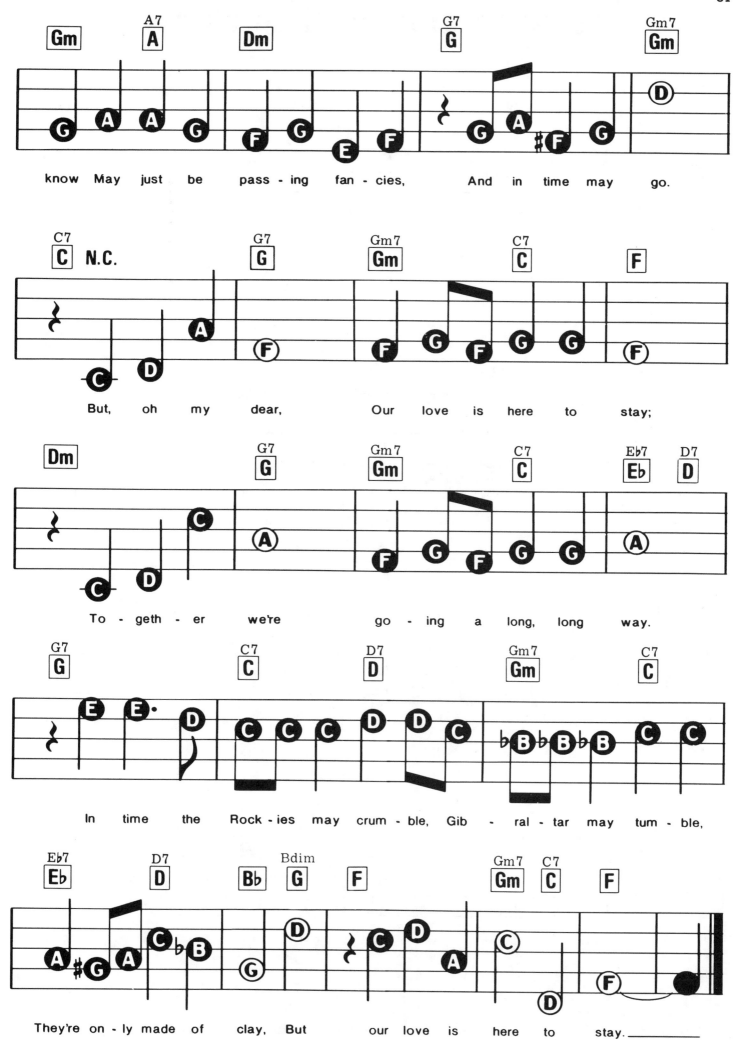

Love Letters In The Sand

Registration 1
Rhythm: Swing

Words by Nick Kenny and Charles Kenny
Music by J. Fred Coots

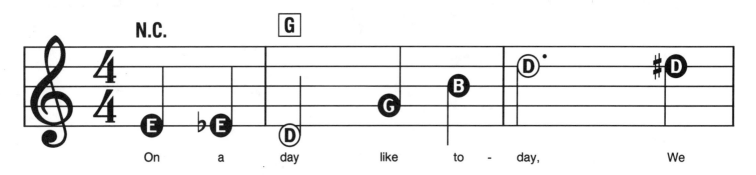

On a day like to - day, We

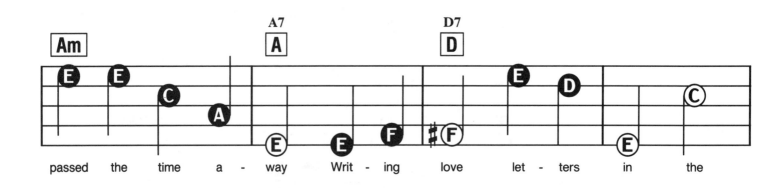

passed the time a - way Writ - ing love let - ters in the

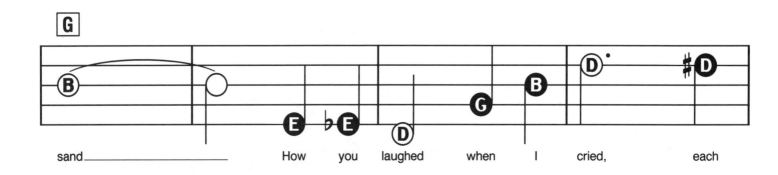

sand_____ How you laughed when I cried, each

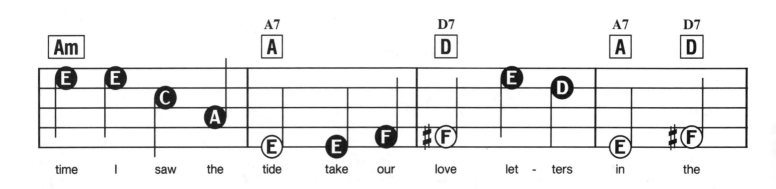

time I saw the tide take our love let - ters in the

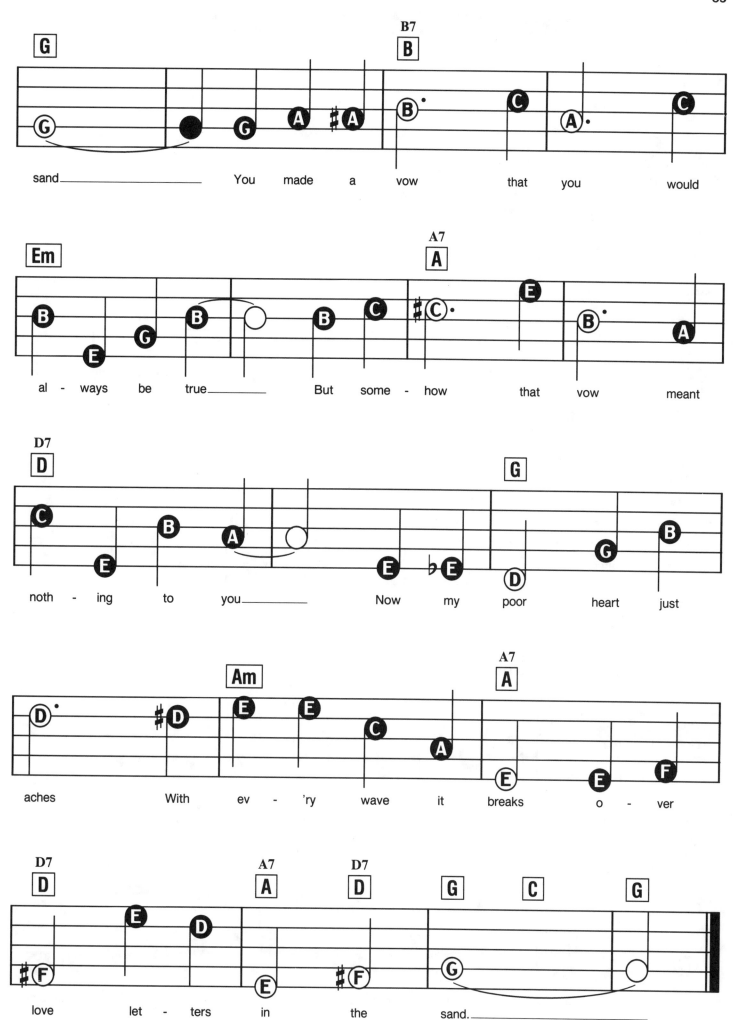

Lullaby Of The Leaves

Registration 10
Rhythm: Fox Trot or Swing

Words by Joe Young
Music by Bernice Petkere

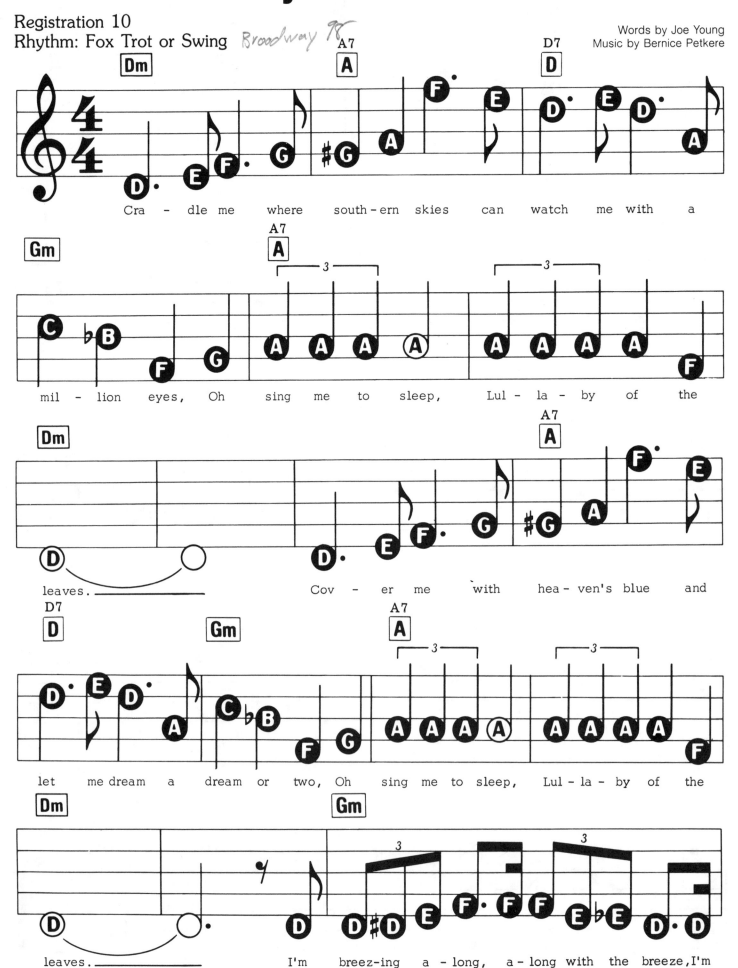

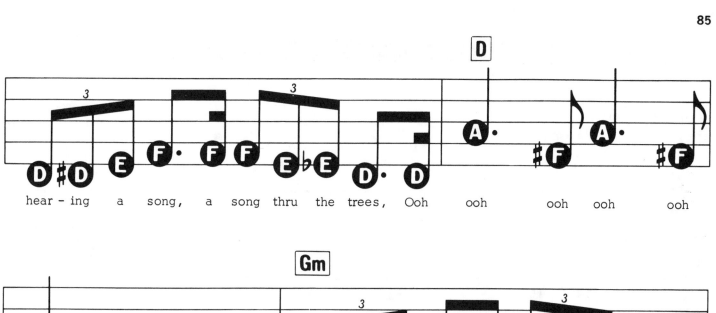

hear - ing a song, a song thru the trees, Ooh ooh ooh ooh ooh

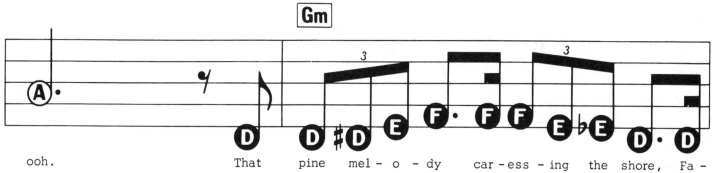

ooh. That pine mel - o - dy car - ess - ing the shore, Fa -

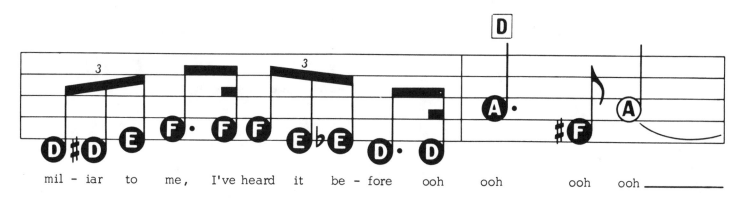

mil - iar to me, I've heard it be - fore ooh ooh ooh ooh _____

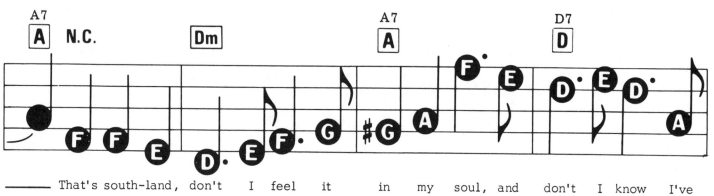

_____ That's south-land, don't I feel it in my soul, and don't I know I've

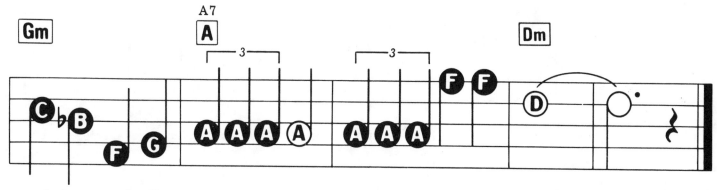

reached my goal, Oh sing me to sleep, Lul - la - by of the leaves._____

Memories Of You

Registration 9
Rhythm: Fox Trot or Swing ~128

Words by Andy Razaf
Music by Eubie Blake

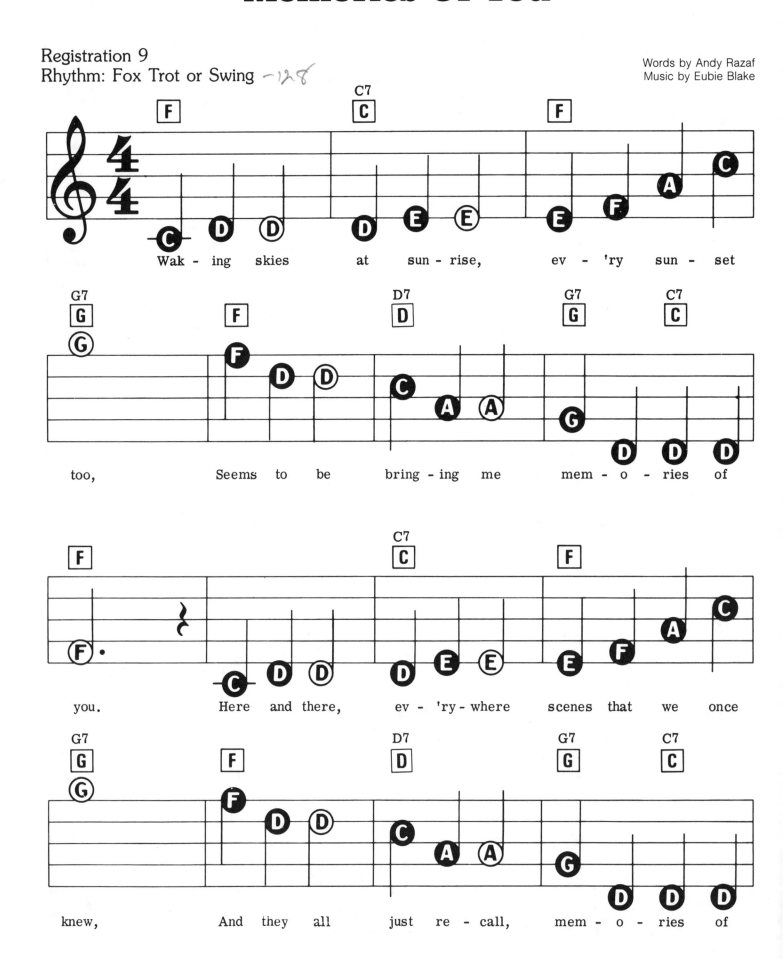

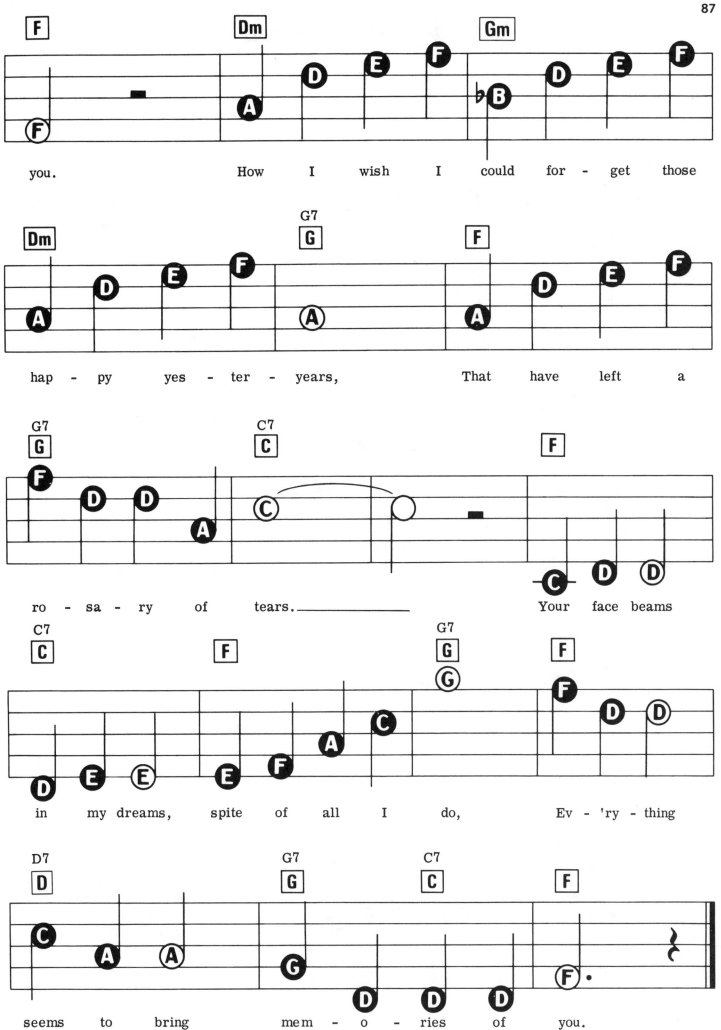

Moon Over Miami

Registration 4
Rhythm: Swing or Jazz *Ballad -80*

Words by Edgar Leslie
Music by Joe Burke

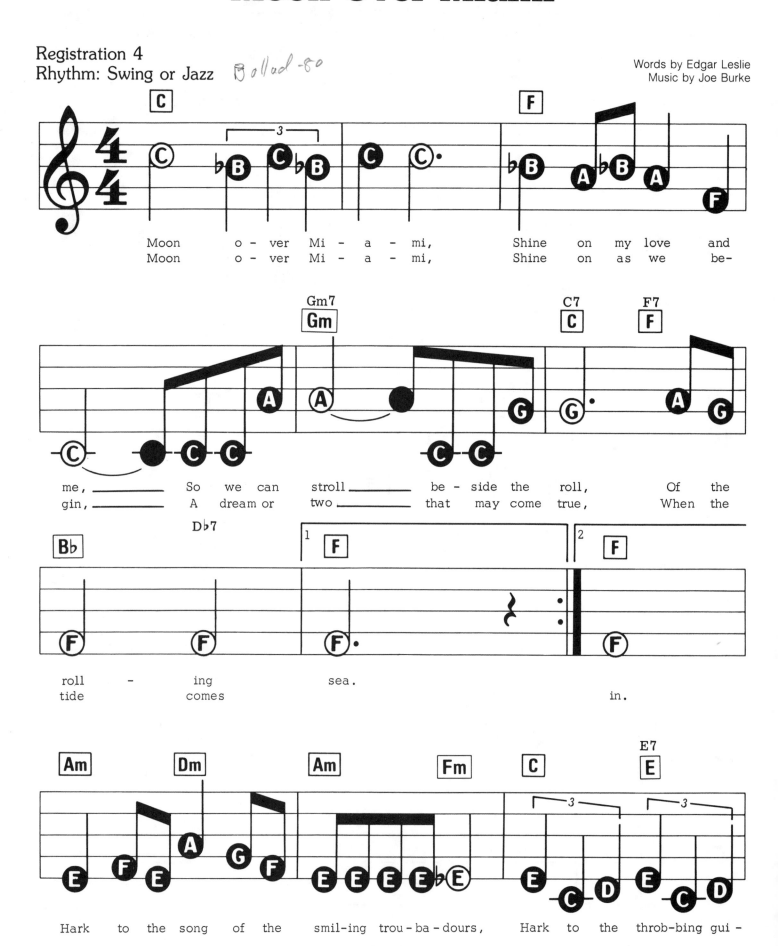

89

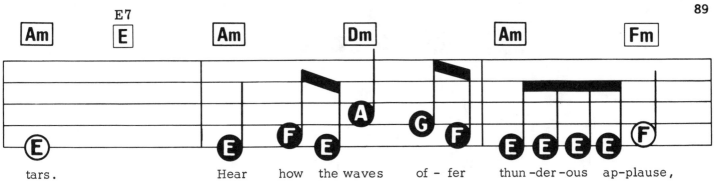

tars.   Hear how the waves of - fer thun -der -ous ap-plause,

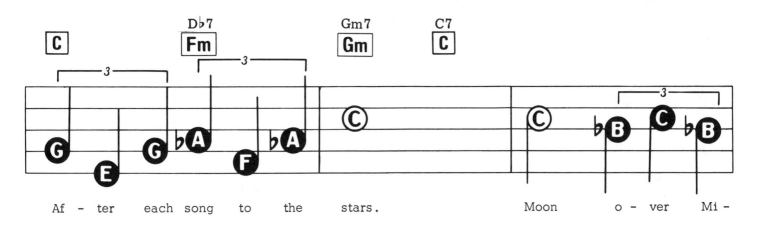

Af – ter each song to the stars.   Moon o - ver Mi –

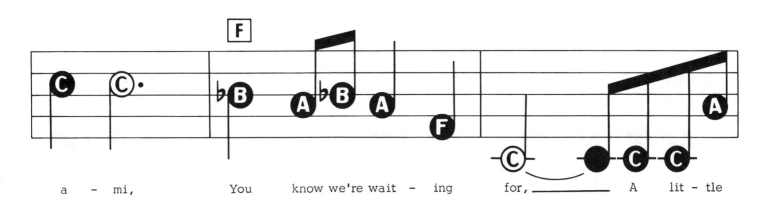

a – mi,   You know we're wait – ing for,_____ A lit - tle

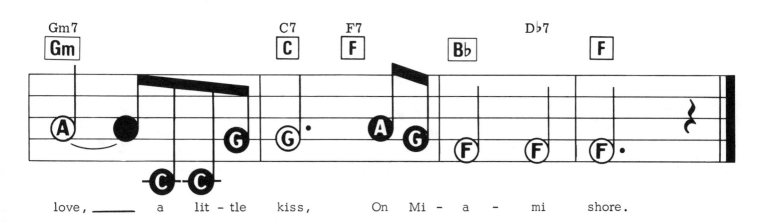

love,_____ a lit - tle kiss, On Mi - a – mi shore.

Moonglow

Registration 2
Rhythm: Fox Trot

BIG BAND 100

Words and Music by Will Hudson,
Eddie DeLange and Irving Mills

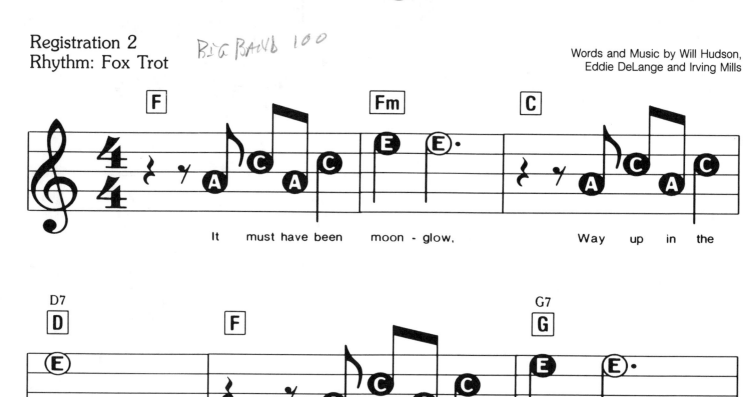

It must have been moon - glow, Way up in the

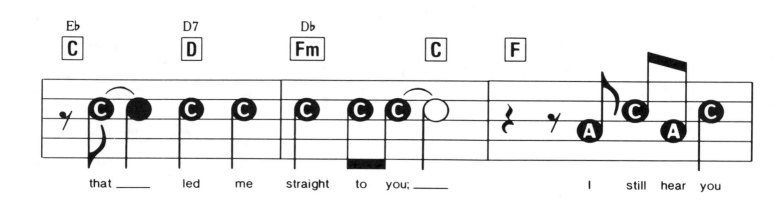

blue, It must have been moon - glow

that ____ led me straight to you; ____ I still hear you

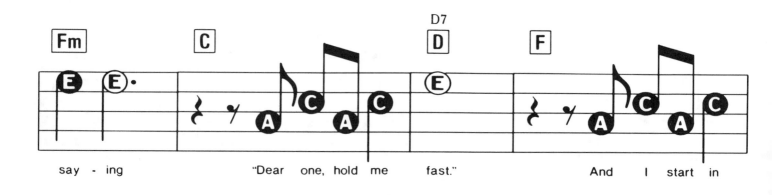

say - ing "Dear one, hold me fast." And I start in

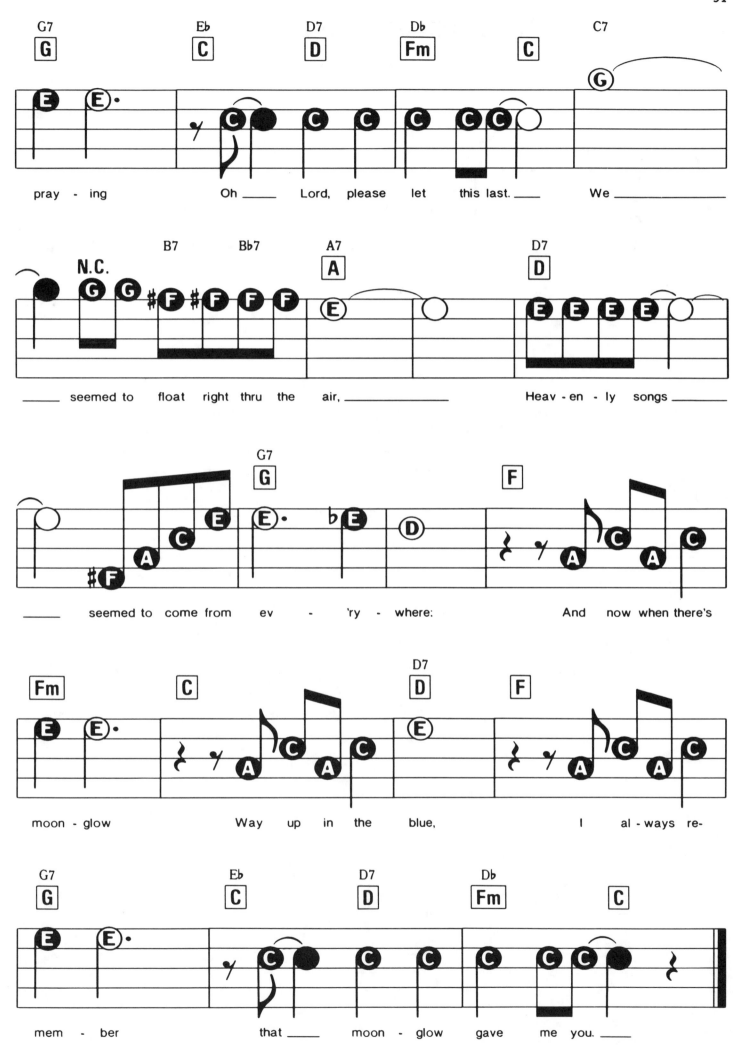

My Funny Valentine

Registration 1
Rhythm: Ballad

Words by Lorenz Hart
Music by Richard Rodgers

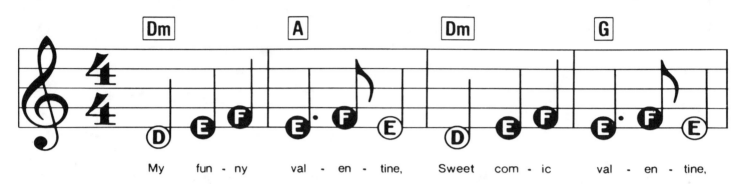

My fun-ny val - en - tine, Sweet com - ic val - en - tine,

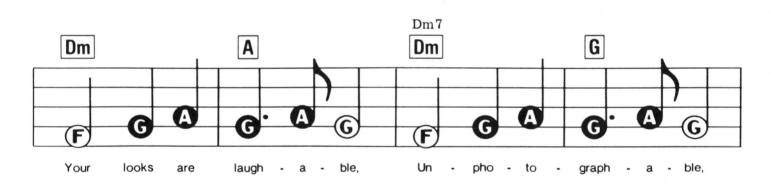

You make me smile with my heart. _____

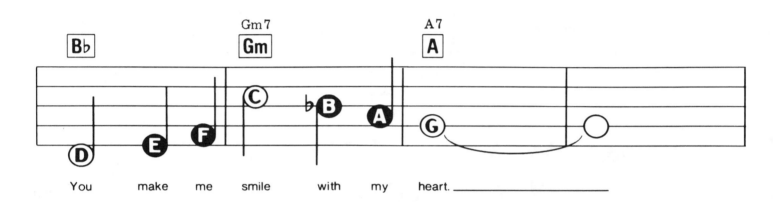

Your looks are laugh - a - ble, Un - pho - to - graph - a - ble,

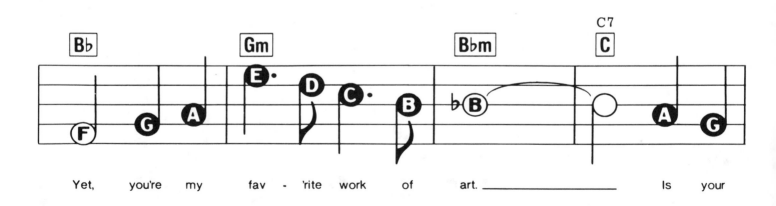

Yet, you're my fav - 'rite work of art. _____ Is your

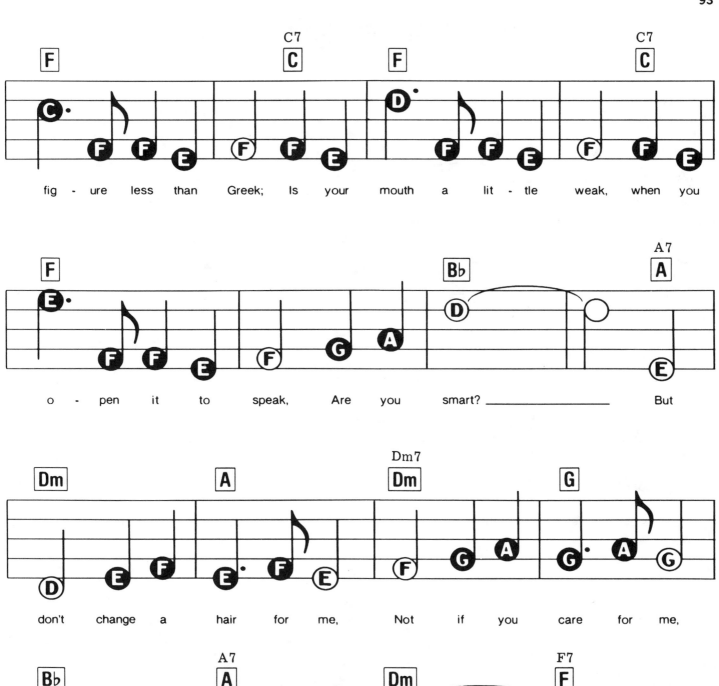

fig - ure less than Greek; Is your mouth a lit - tle weak, when you

o - pen it to speak, Are you smart? _____ But

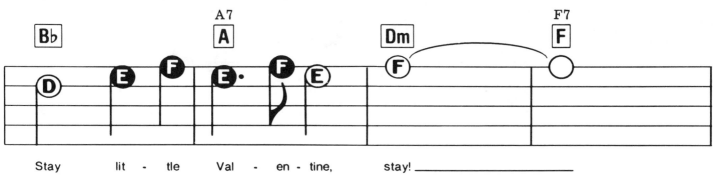

don't change a hair for me, Not if you care for me,

Stay lit - tle Val - en - tine, stay! _____

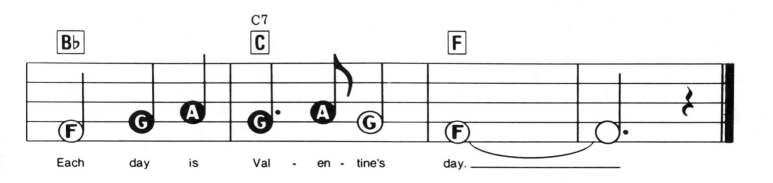

Each day is Val - en - tine's day. _____

My Prayer

Registration 3
Rhythm: Fox Trot or Swing

Music by Georges Boulanger
Lyric and Musical Adaptation by Jimmy Kennedy

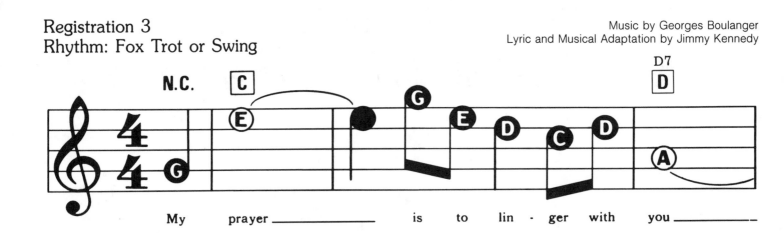

My prayer _____ is to lin - ger with you _____

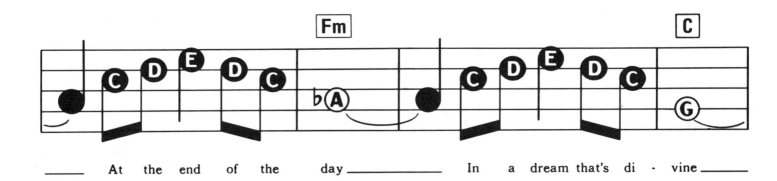

_____ At the end of the day _____ In a dream that's di - vine _____

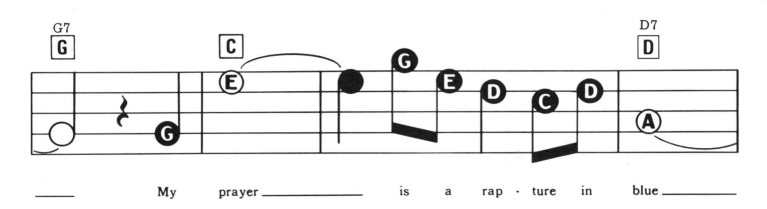

_____ My prayer _____ is a rap - ture in blue _____

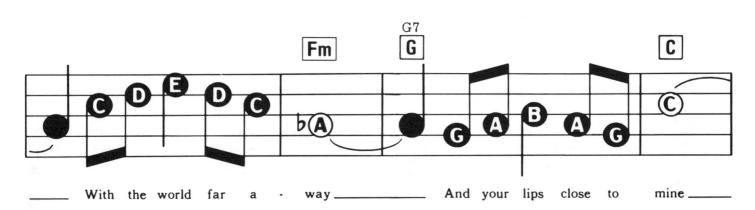

_____ With the world far a - way _____ And your lips close to mine _____

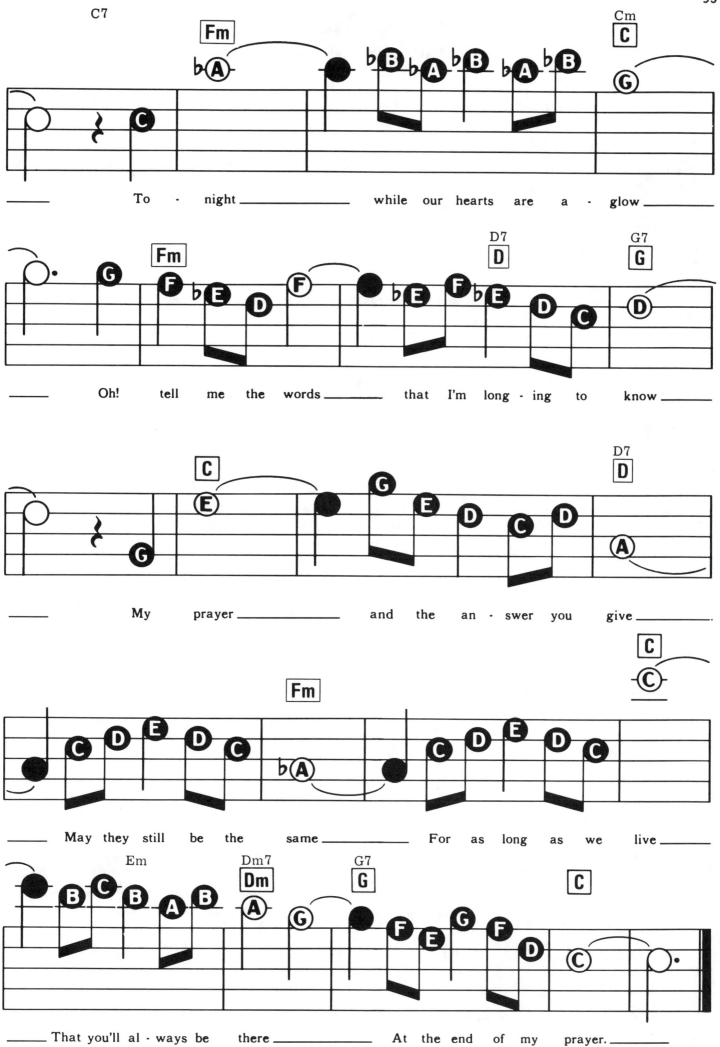

Nevertheless
(I'm In Love With You)

Registration 4
Rhythm: Fox Trot or Ballad

Words and Music by
Bert Kalmar and Harry Ruby

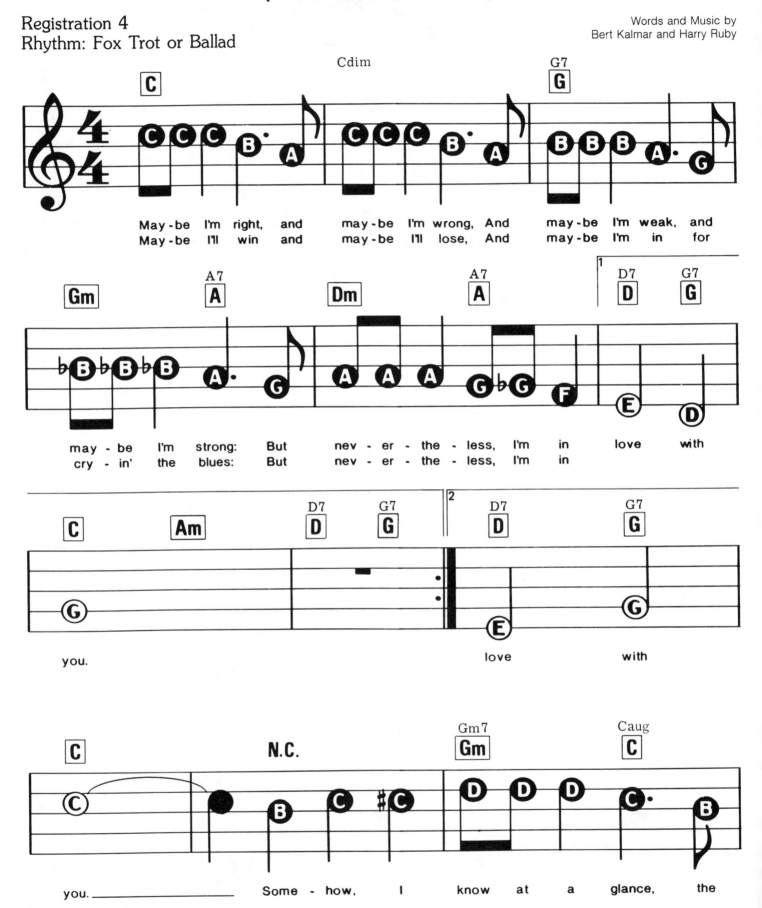

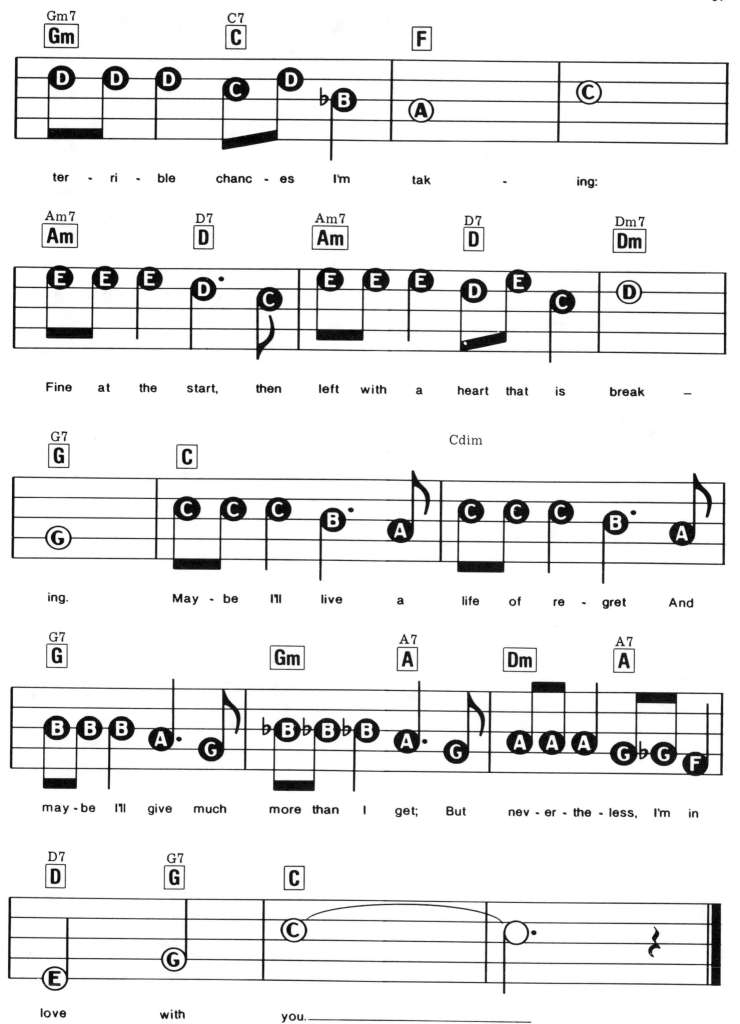

Nice Work If You Can Get It

(From "A DAMSEL IN DISTRESS")

Registration 7
Rhythm: Swing

Words by Ira Gershwin
Music by George Gershwin

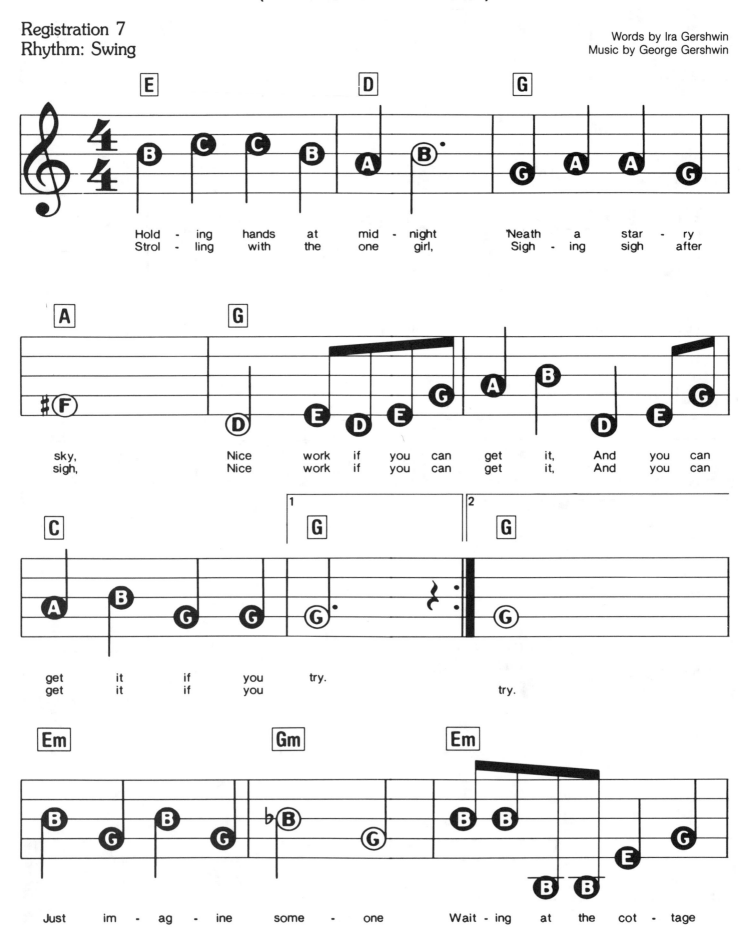

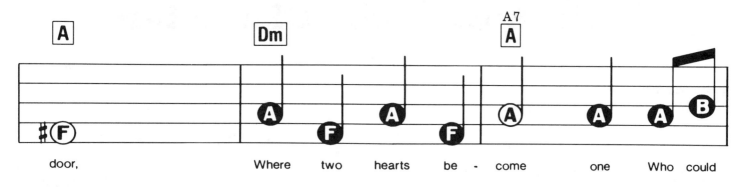

door,   Where two   hearts be - come   one   Who could

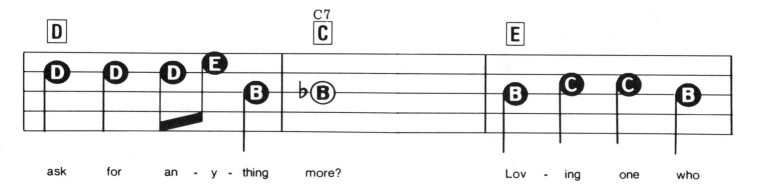

ask   for   an - y - thing   more?   Lov - ing   one   who

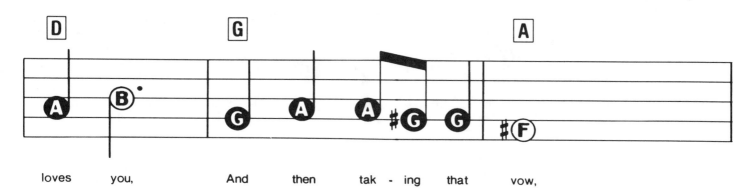

loves   you,   And   then   tak - ing   that   vow,

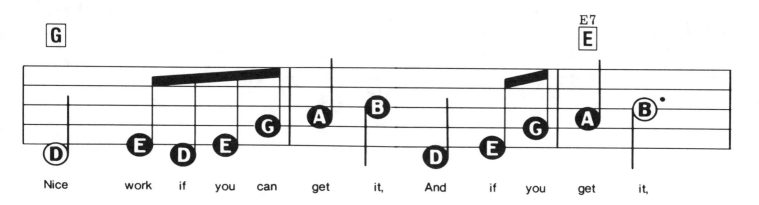

Nice   work   if   you   can   get   it,   And   if   you   get   it,

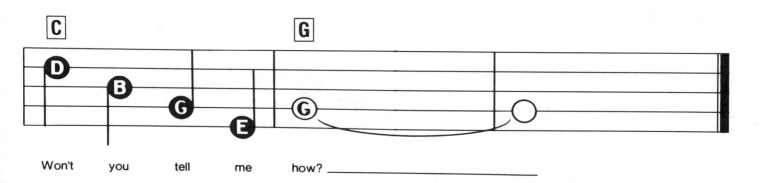

Won't   you   tell   me   how? _____

On The Sunny Side Of The Street

Registration 7
Rhythm: Fox Trot or Swing

Lyric by Dorothy Fields
Music by Jimmy McHugh

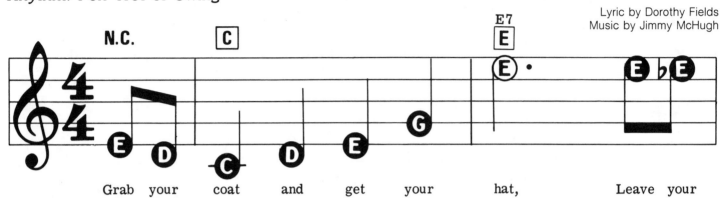

Grab your coat and get your hat, Leave your

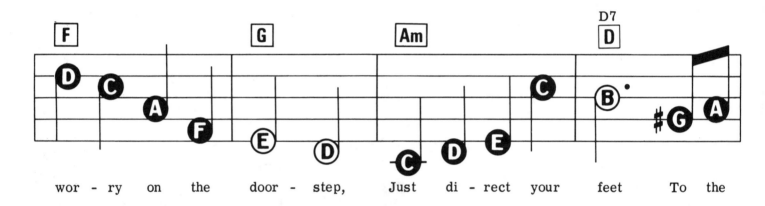

wor - ry on the door - step, Just di - rect your feet To the

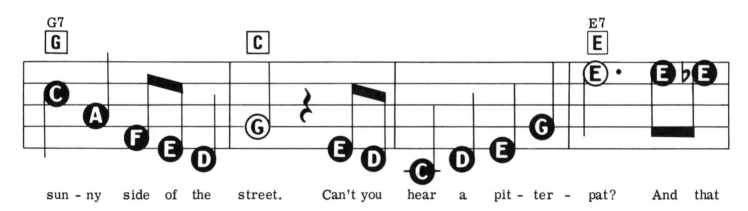

sun - ny side of the street. Can't you hear a pit - ter - pat? And that

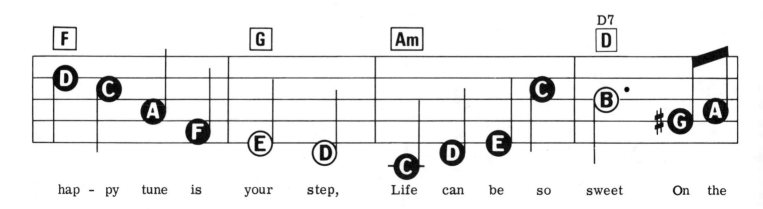

hap - py tune is your step, Life can be so sweet On the

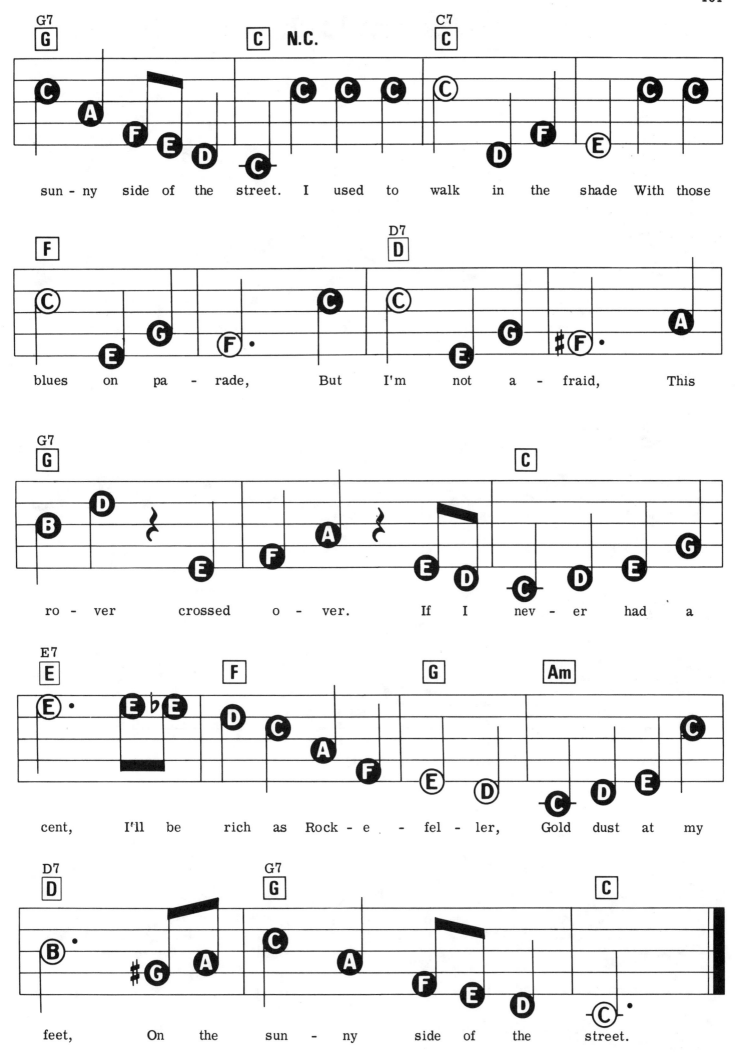

Paper Doll

Registration 4
Rhythm: Fox Trot or Swing

By Johnny S. Black

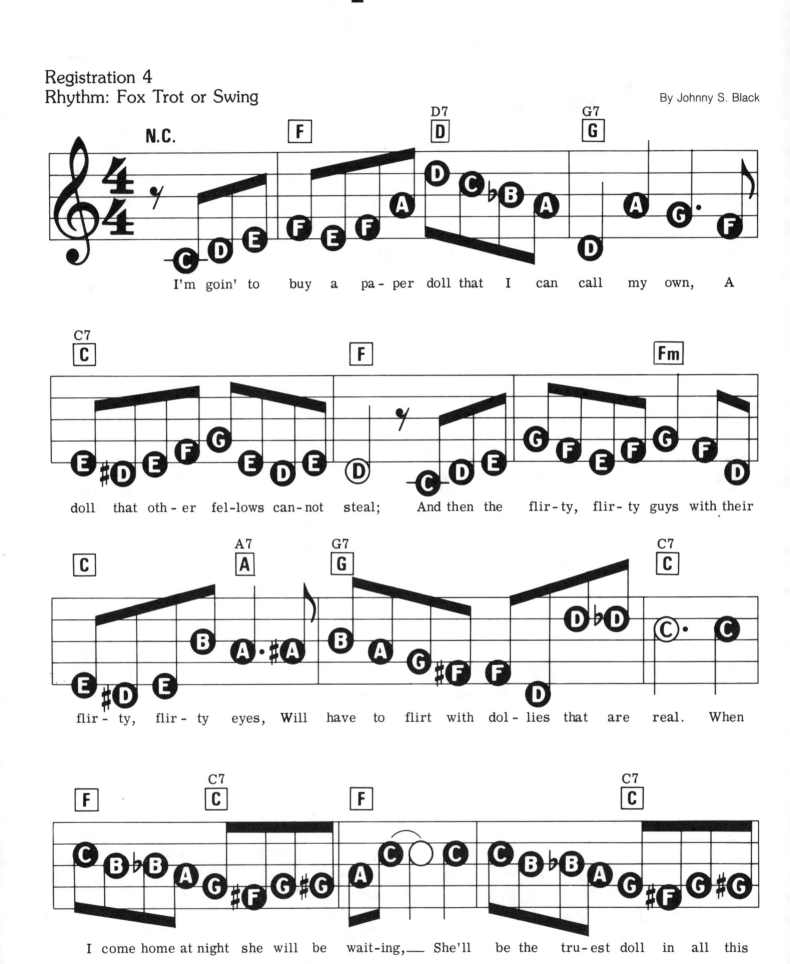

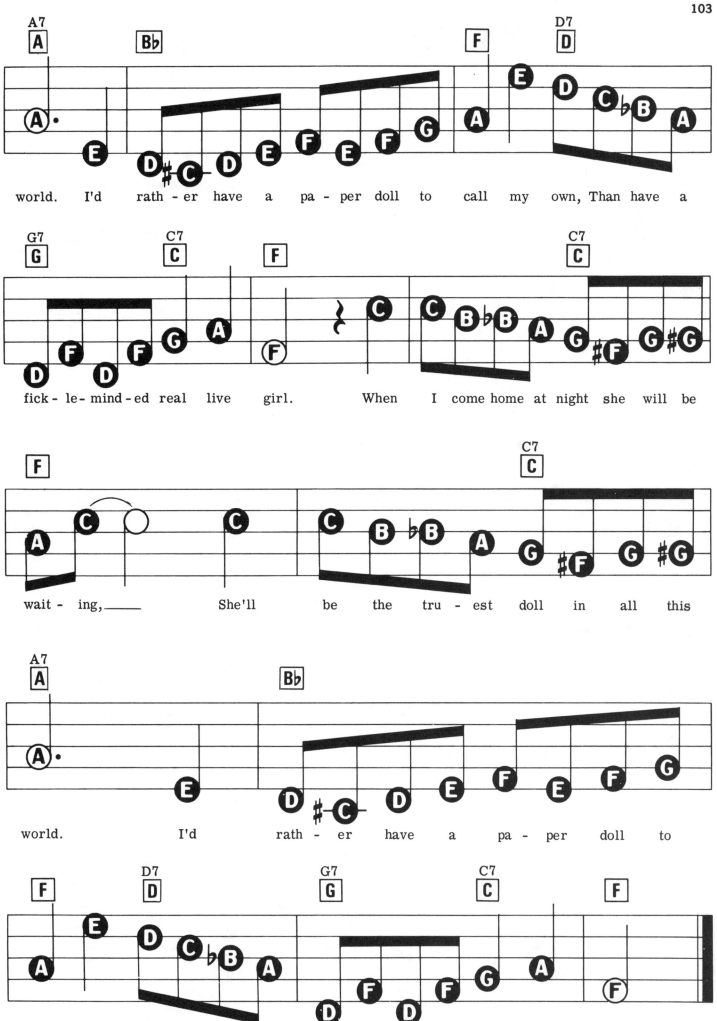

Pennies From Heaven

Registration 2
Rhythm: Fox Trot or Swing

Words by John Burke
Music by Arthur Johnston

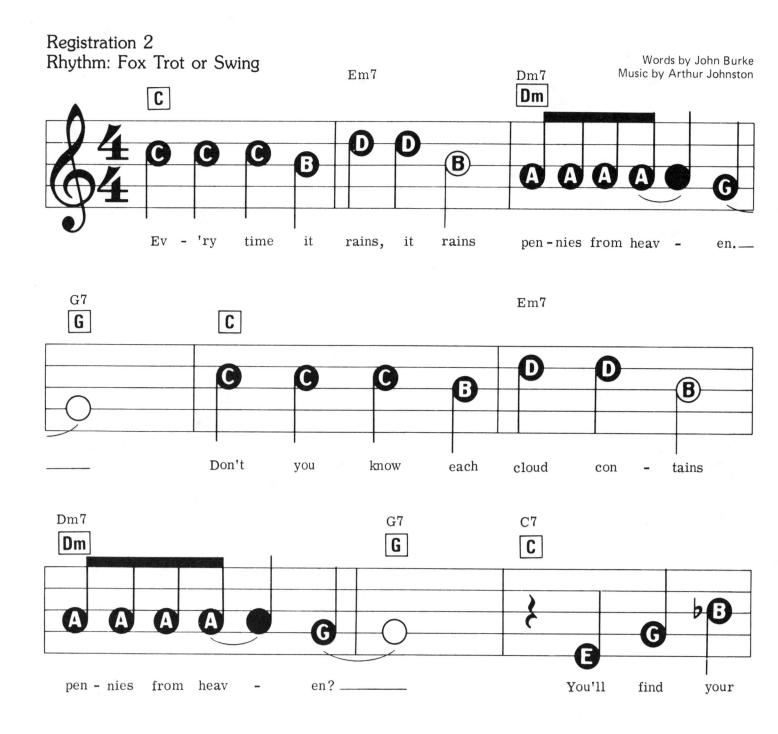

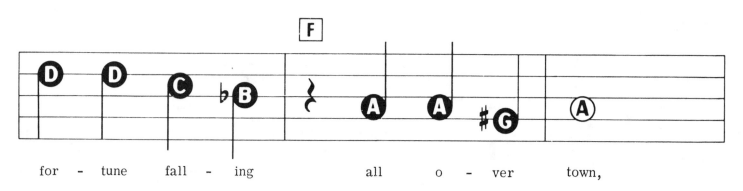

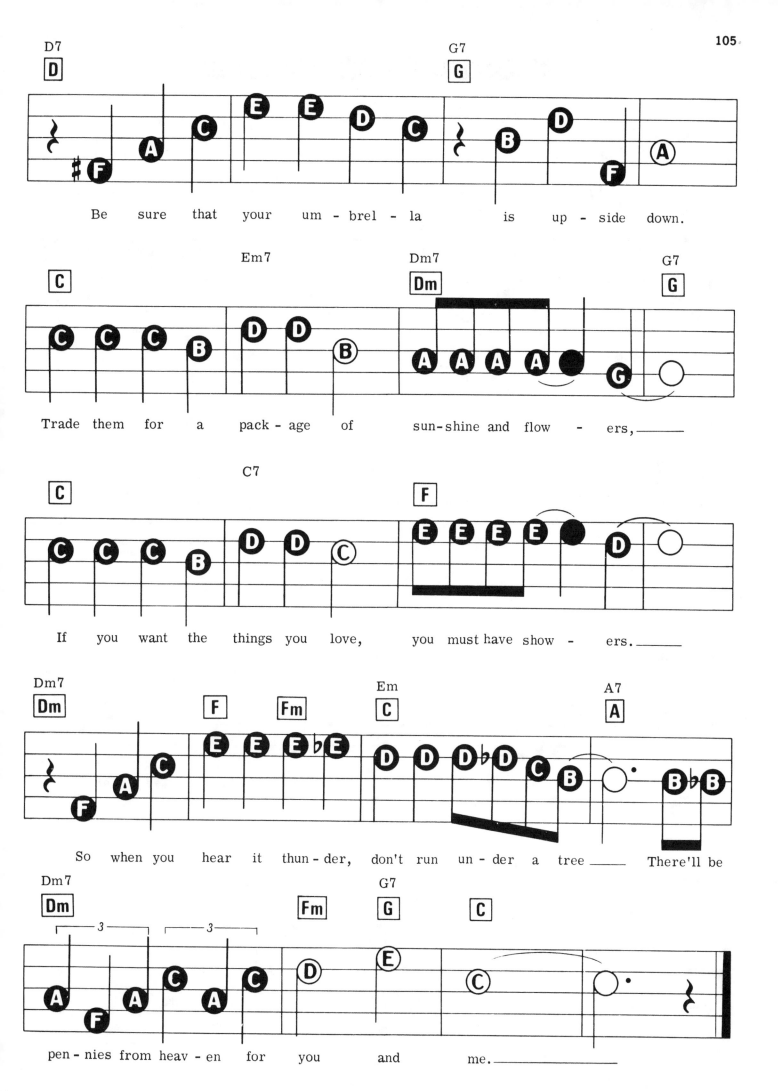

Red Sails In The Sunset

Registration 3
Rhythm: Fox Trot or Ballad

Words by Jimmy Kennedy
Music by Hugh Williams

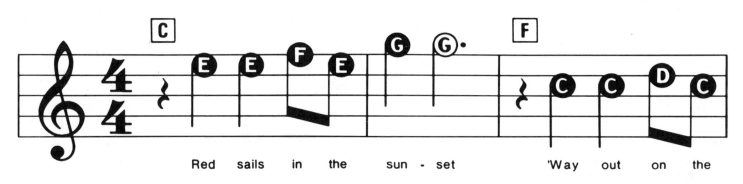

Red sails in the sun - set   'Way out on the

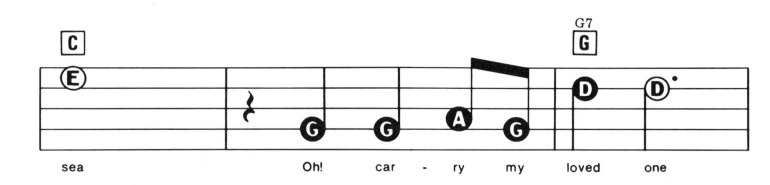

sea   Oh!   car - ry   my   loved   one

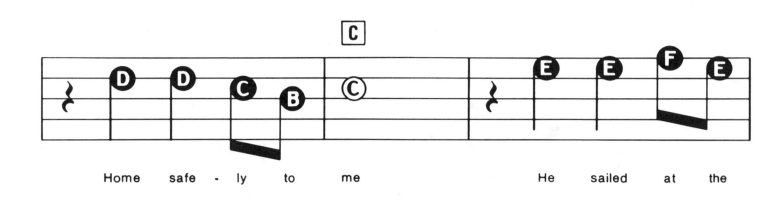

Home safe - ly to me   He   sailed   at   the

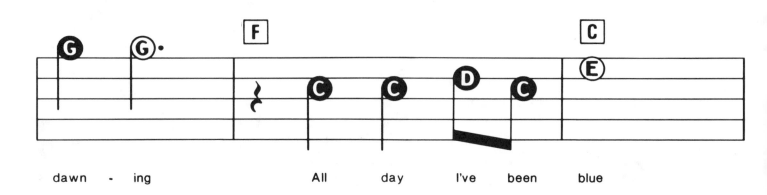

dawn - ing   All   day   I've   been   blue

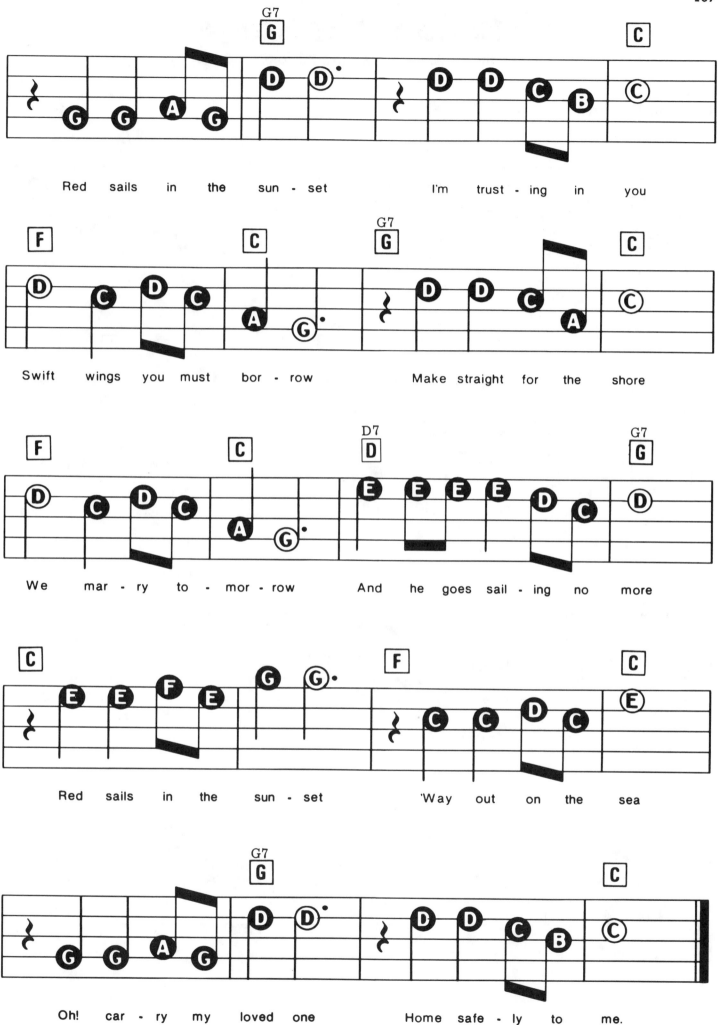

September Song

(From the Musical Play "KNICKERBOCKER HOLIDAY")

Registration 2
Rhythm: Fox Trot

Words by Maxwell Anderson
Music by Kurt Weill

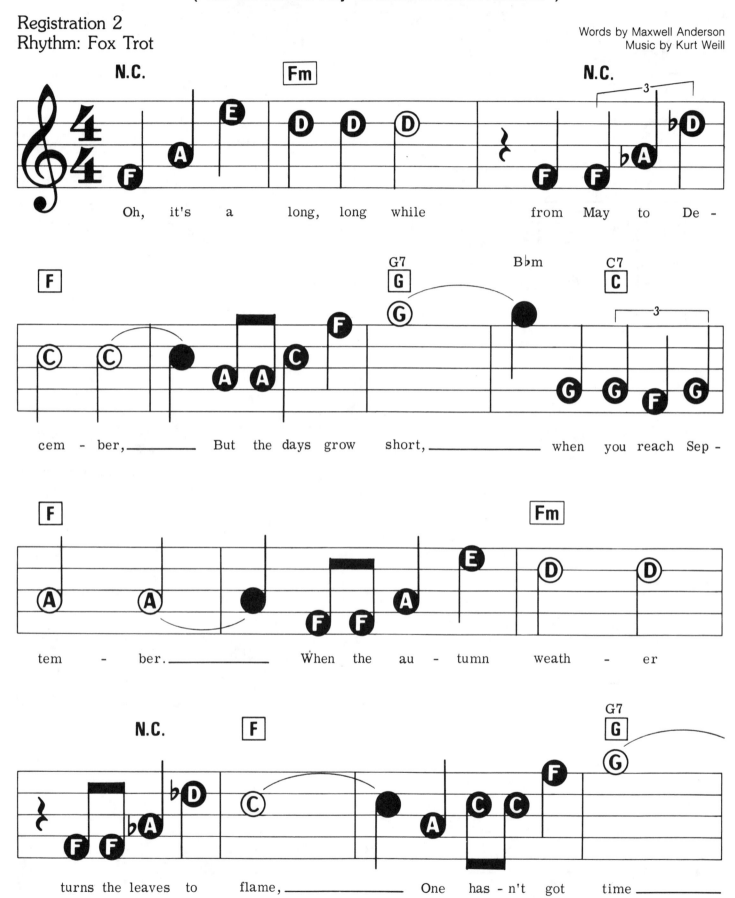

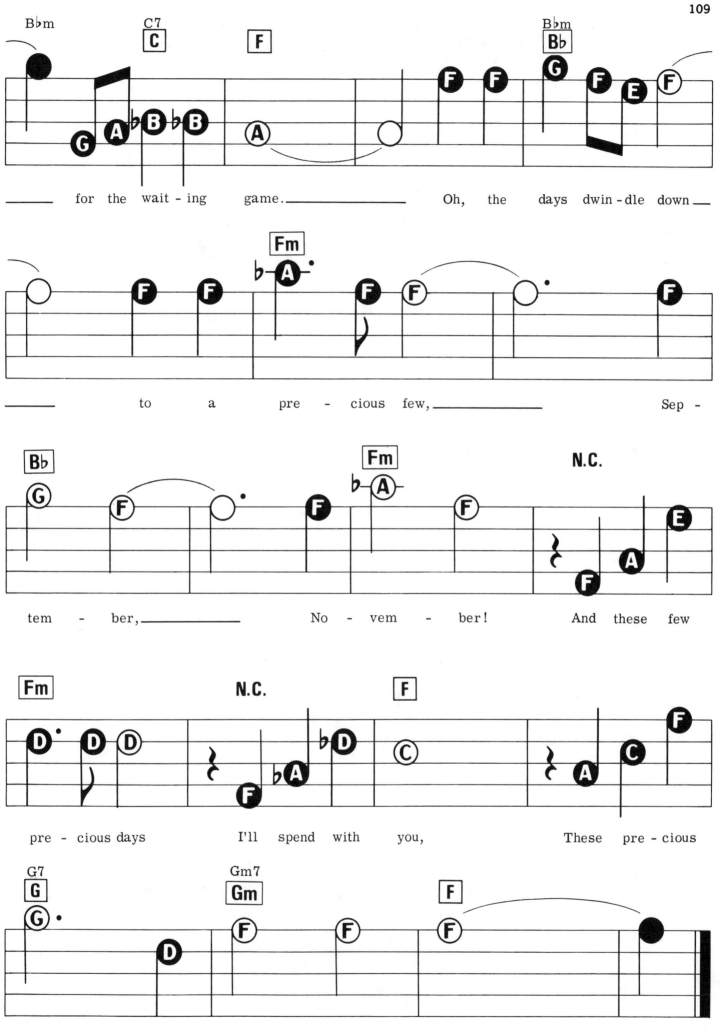

Smoke Gets In Your Eyes

Registration 10
Rhythm: Ballad or Swing

Words by Otto Harbach
Music by Jerome Kern

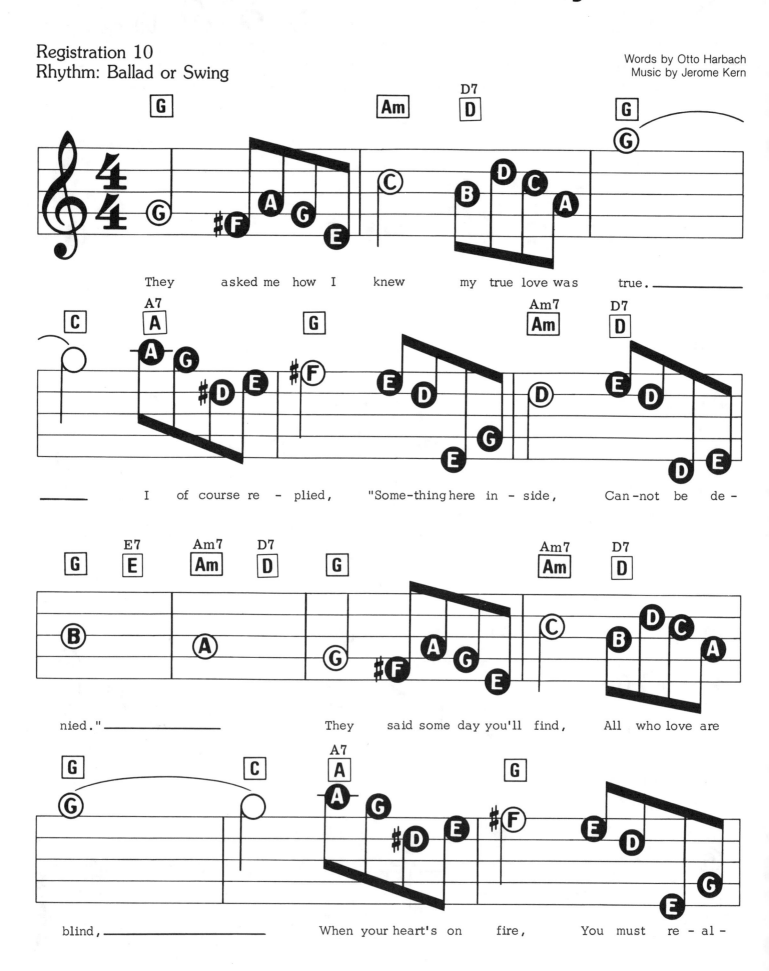

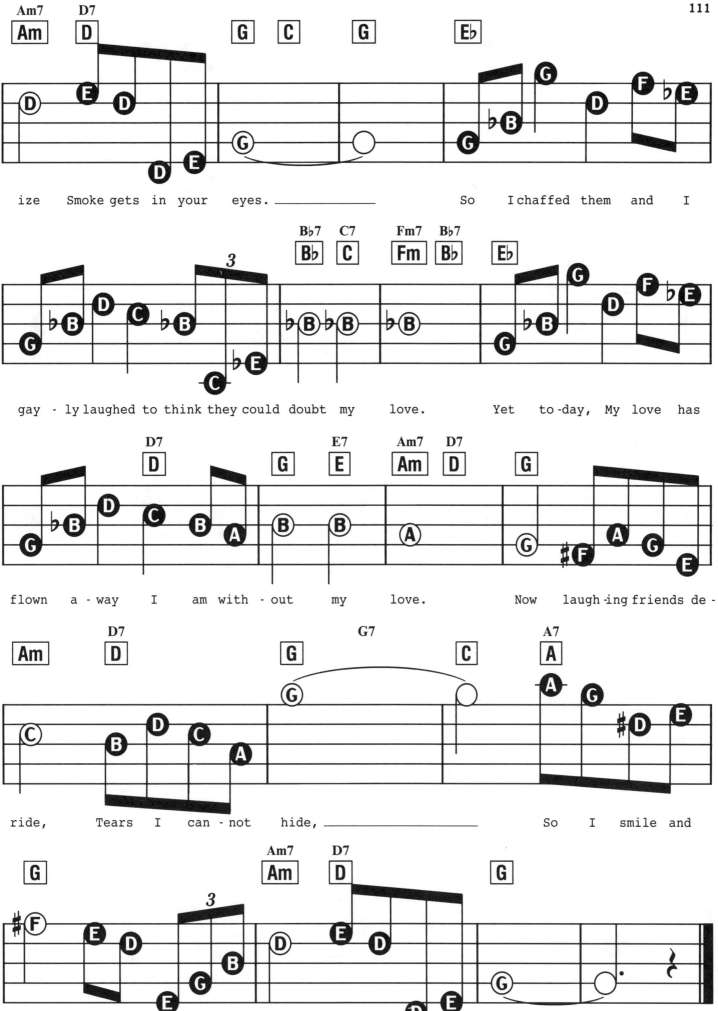

Some Day My Prince Will Come

(From "SNOW WHITE AND THE SEVEN DWARFS")

Registration 2
Rhythm: Waltz

Words by Larry Morey
Music by Frank Churchill

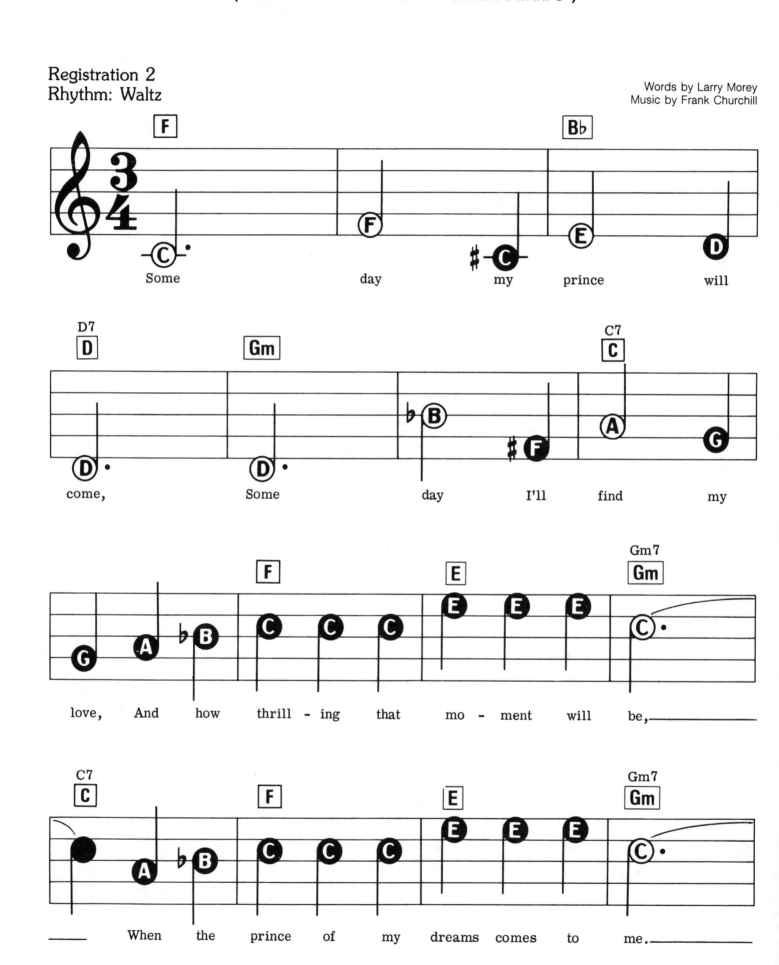

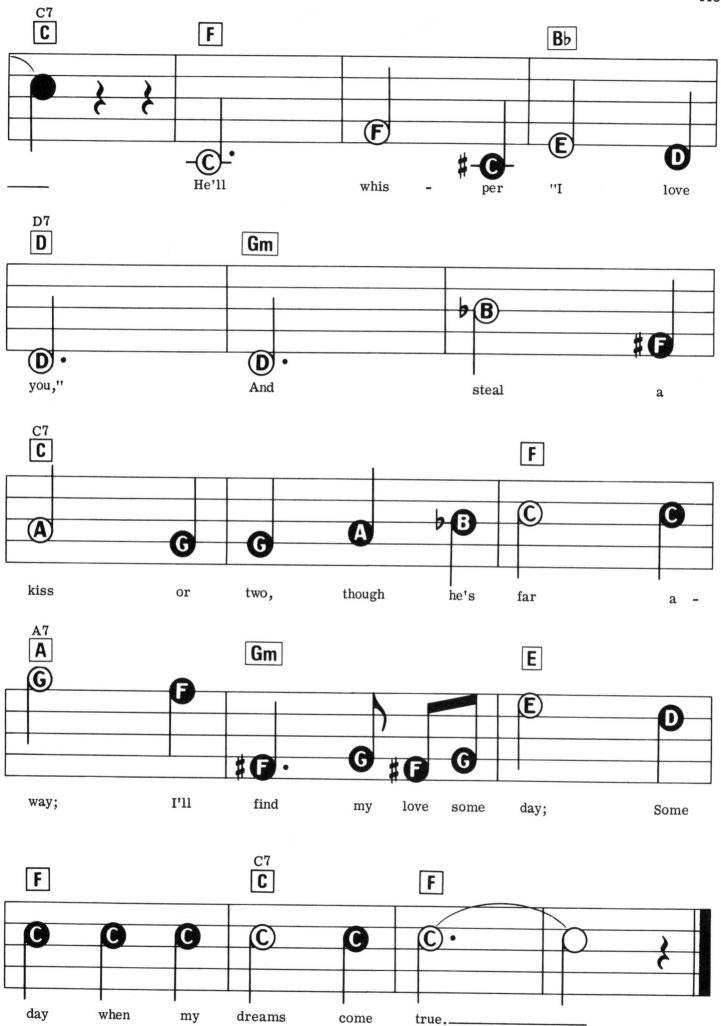

Summertime

Registration 10
Rhythm: Ballad or Blues

Words by DuBose Heyward
Music by George Gershwin

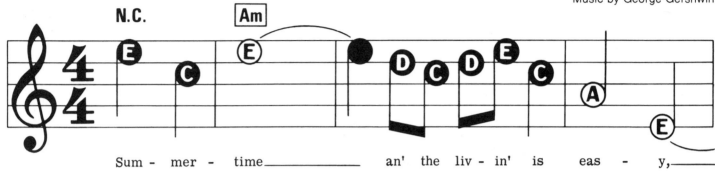

Sum - mer - time _____ an' the liv - in' is eas - y, _____

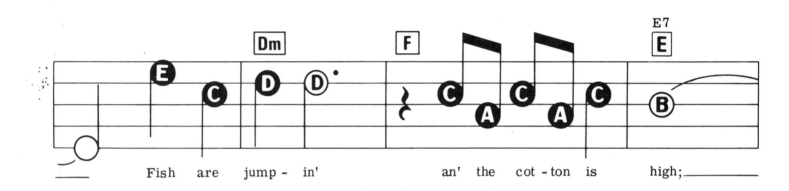

Fish are jump - in' an' the cot - ton is high; _____

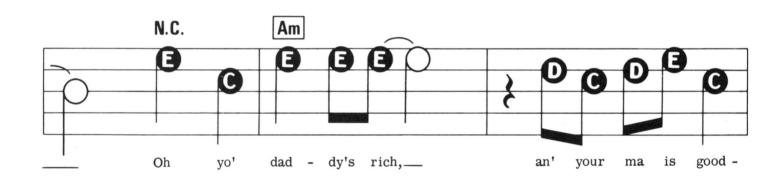

Oh yo' dad - dy's rich, _____ an' your ma is good -

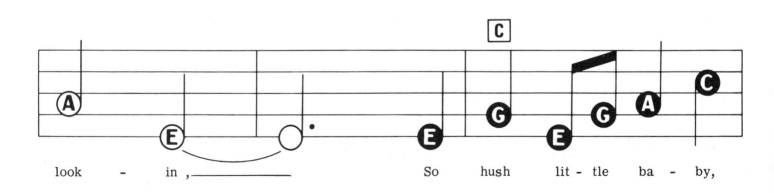

look - in, _____ So hush lit - tle ba - by,

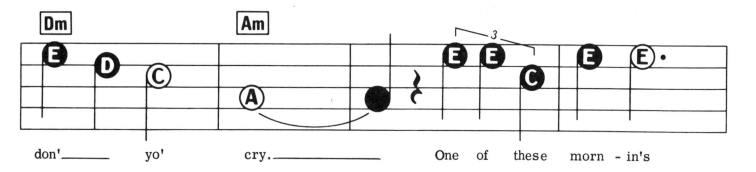

don'_____ yo' cry._____ One of these morn - in's

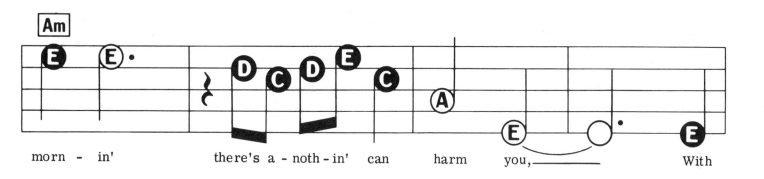

you goin' to rise____ up sing - in',_____ Then you'll

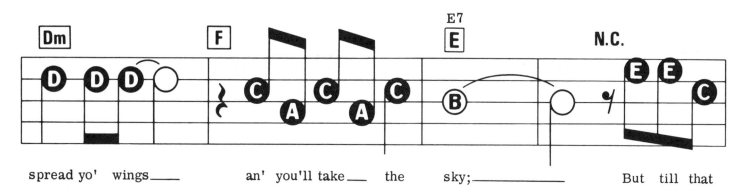

spread yo' wings____ an' you'll take__ the sky;_____ But till that

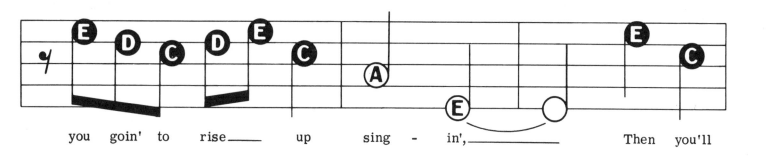

morn - in' there's a - noth - in' can harm you,_____ With

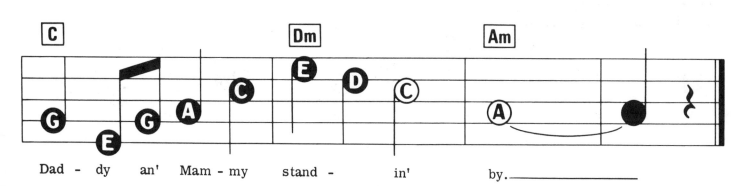

Dad - dy an' Mam - my stand - in' by._____

That's My Desire

Registration 2
Rhythm: Swing

Words by Carroll Loveday
Music by Helmy Kresa

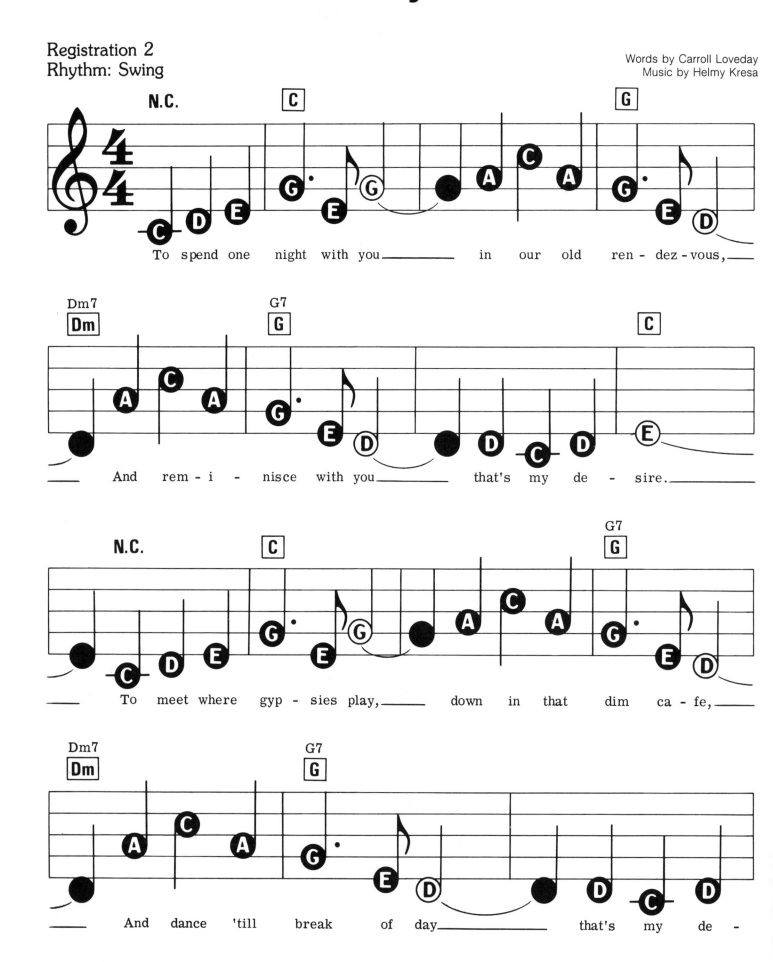

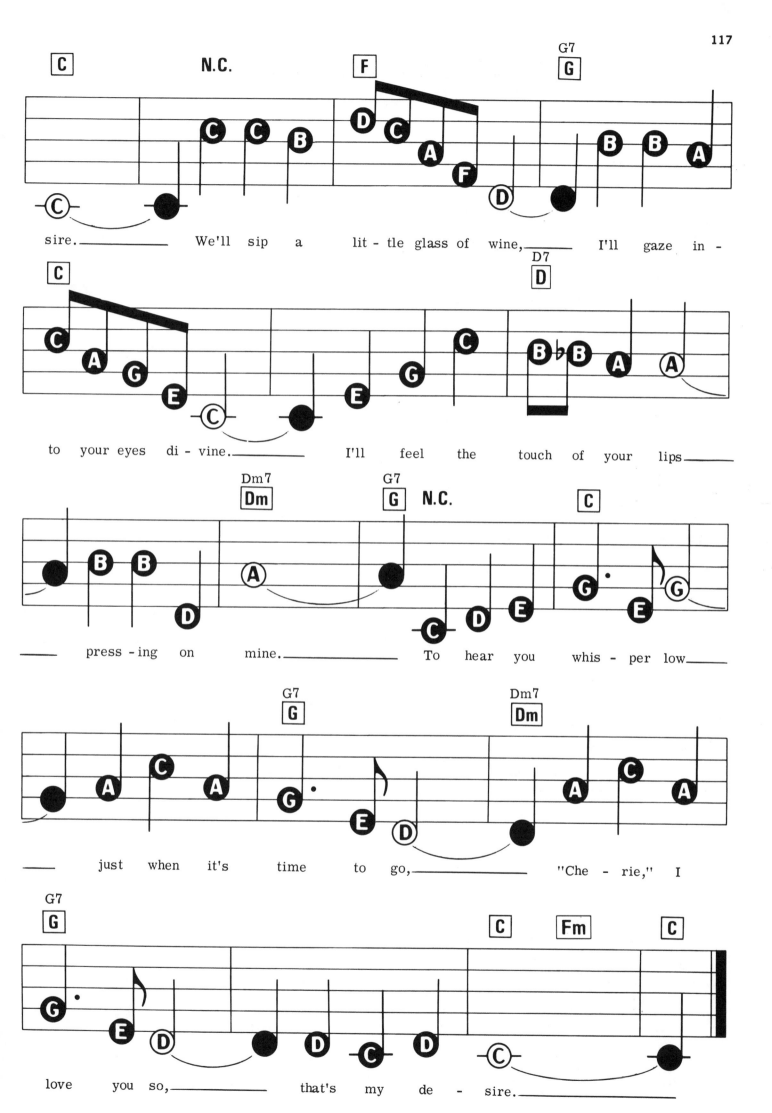

These Foolish Things
(Remind Me Of You)

Registration 9
Rhythm: Fox Trot

Words by Holt Marvell
Music by Jack Strachey and Harry Link

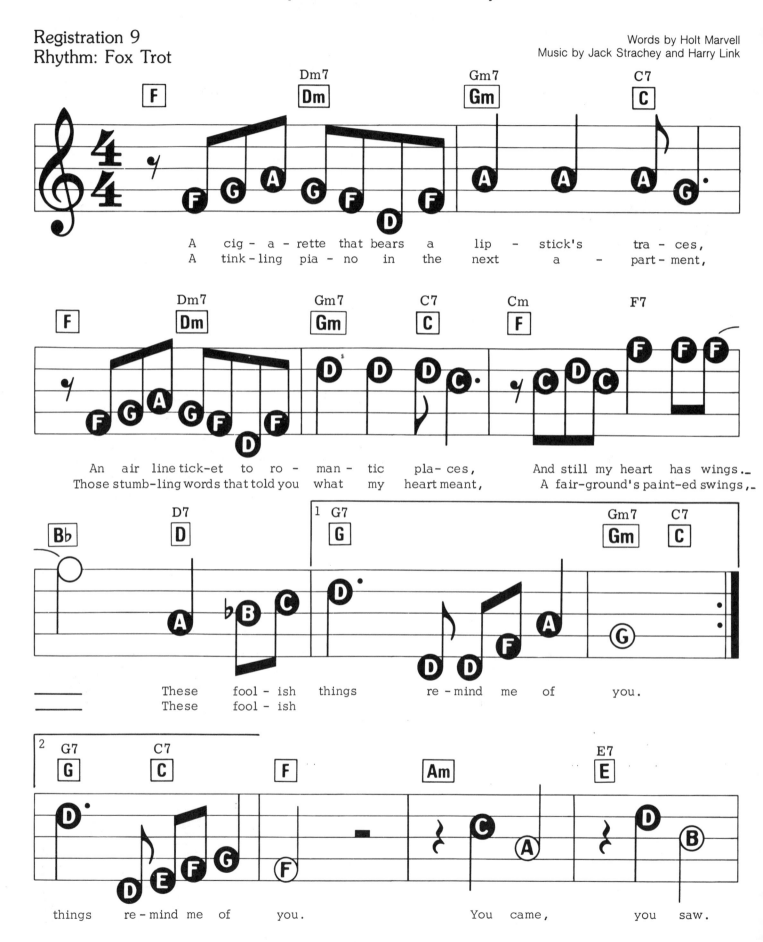

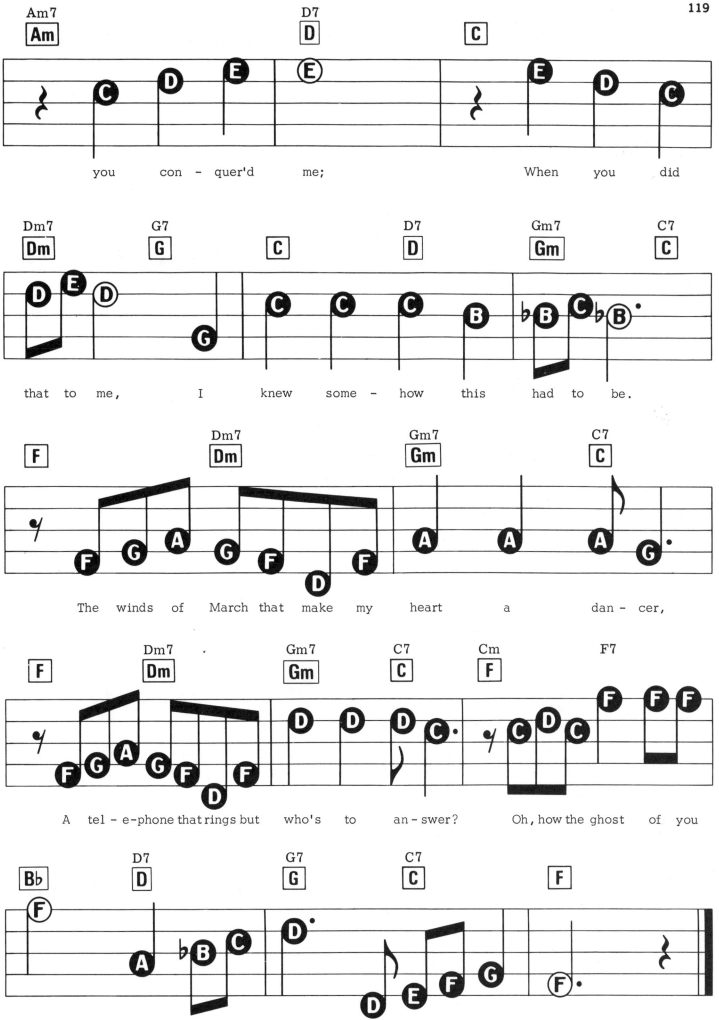

They Can't Take That Away From Me

Registration 1
Rhythm: Fox Trot or Ballad

Words by Ira Gershwin
Music by George Gershwin

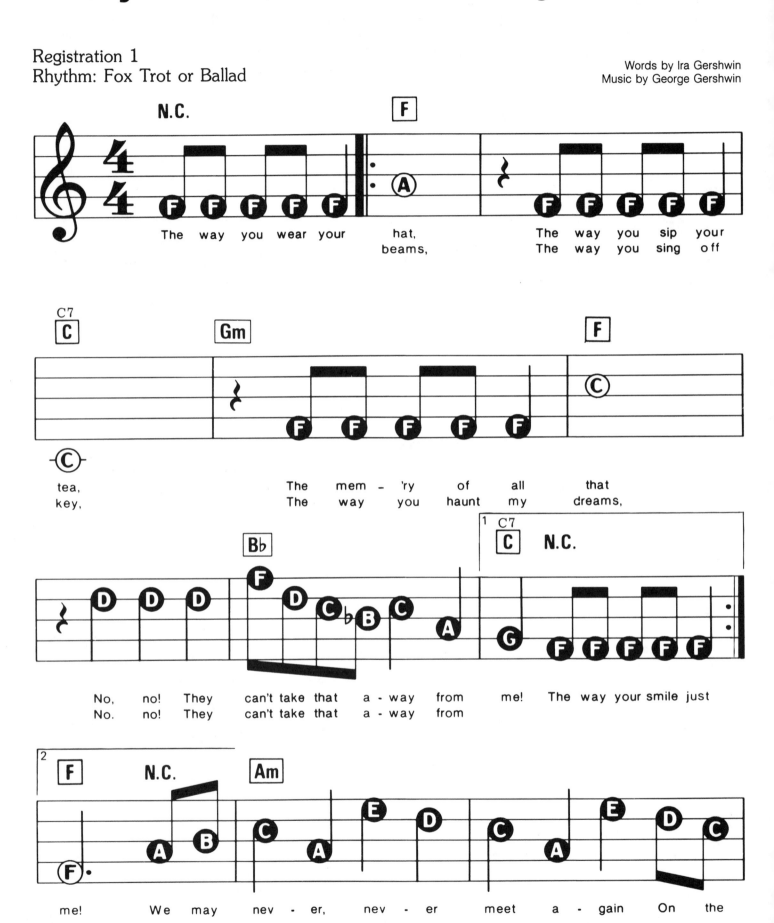

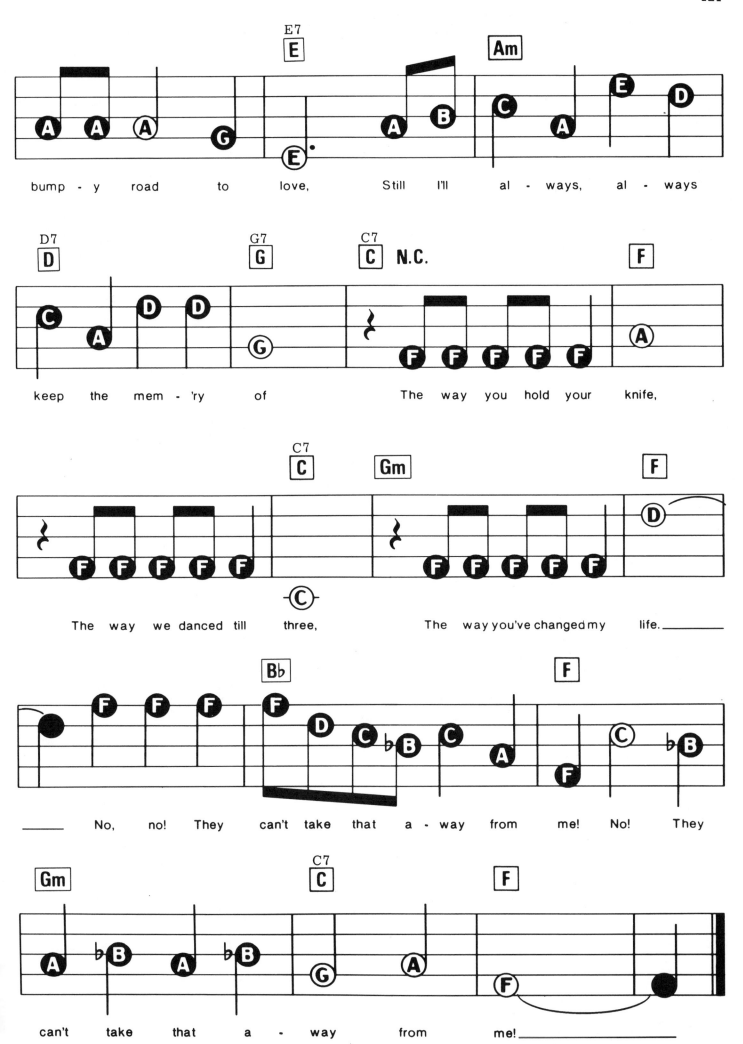

This Can't Be Love
(From "THE BOYS FROM SYRACUSE")

Registration 1
Rhythm: Swing or Jazz

Words by Lorenz Hart
Music by Richard Rodgers

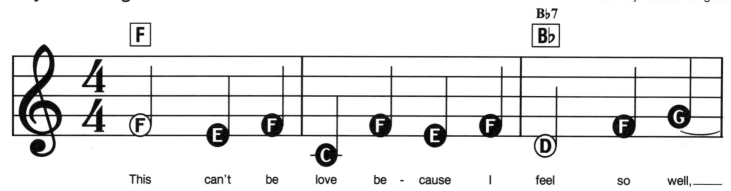

This can't be love be - cause I feel so well,

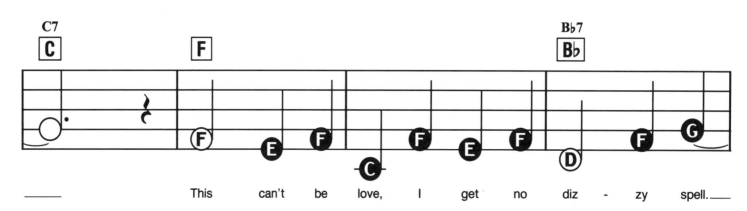

No sobs, no sor - rows, no sighs;

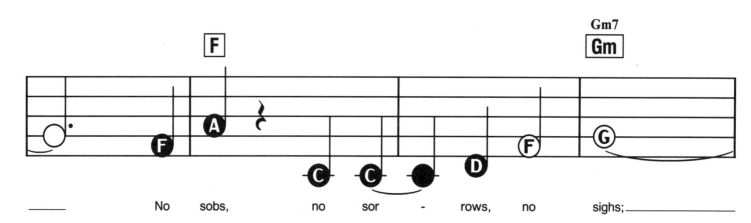

This can't be love, I get no diz - zy spell.

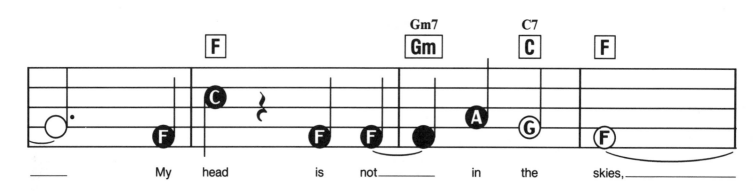

My head is not in the skies,

123

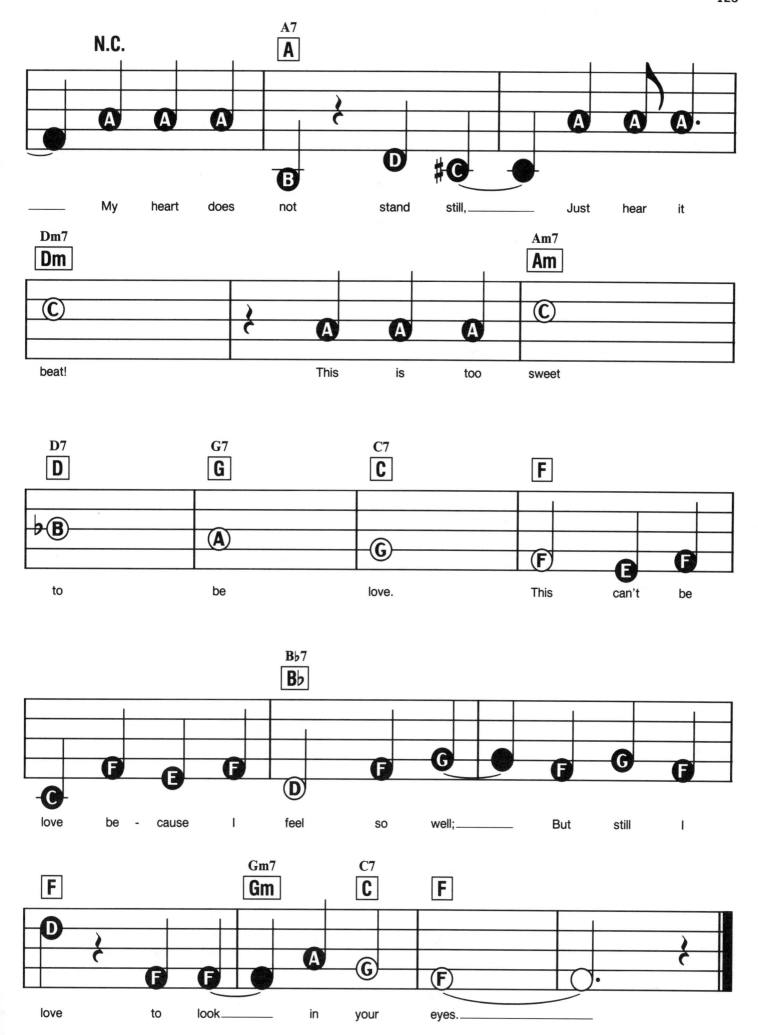

Under A Blanket Of Blue

Registration 3
Rhythm: Swing

Words by Marty Symes and Al J. Neiburg
Music by Jerry Livingston

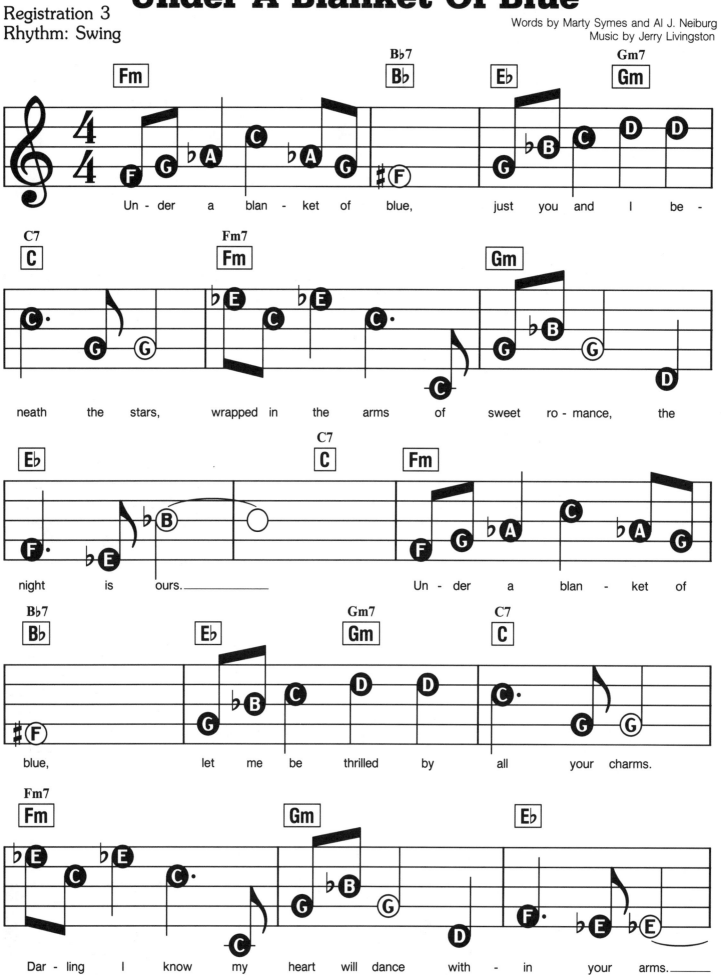

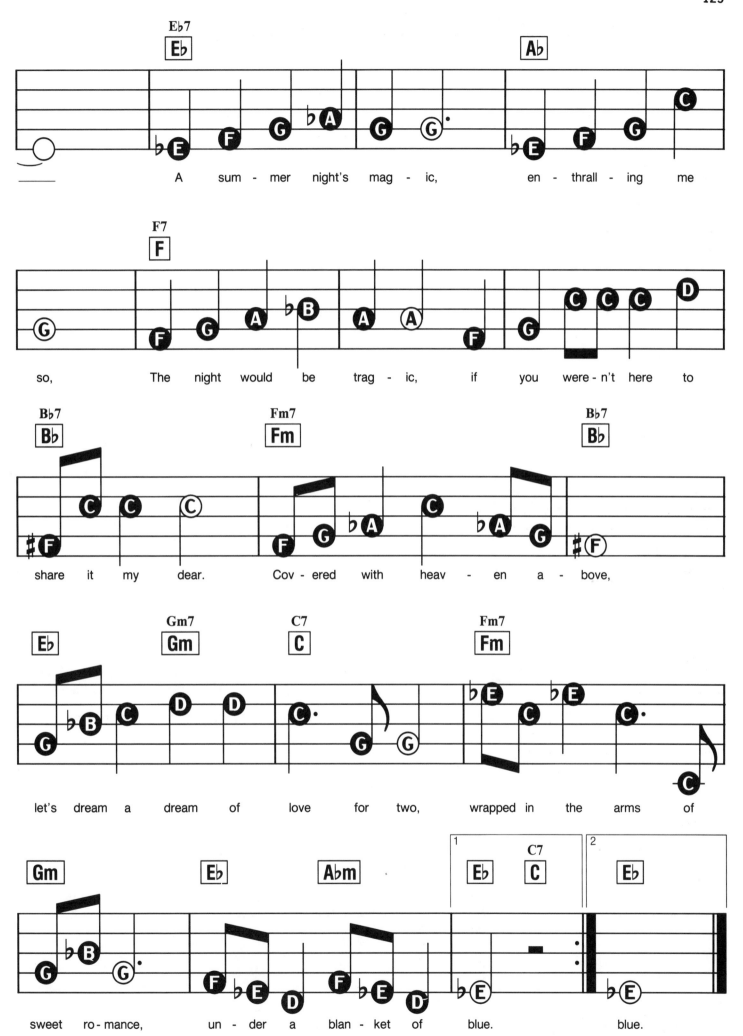

What A Diff'rence A Day Made

Registration 8
Rhythm: Latin or Rhumba

Lyrics by Stanley Adams
Music by Maria Grever

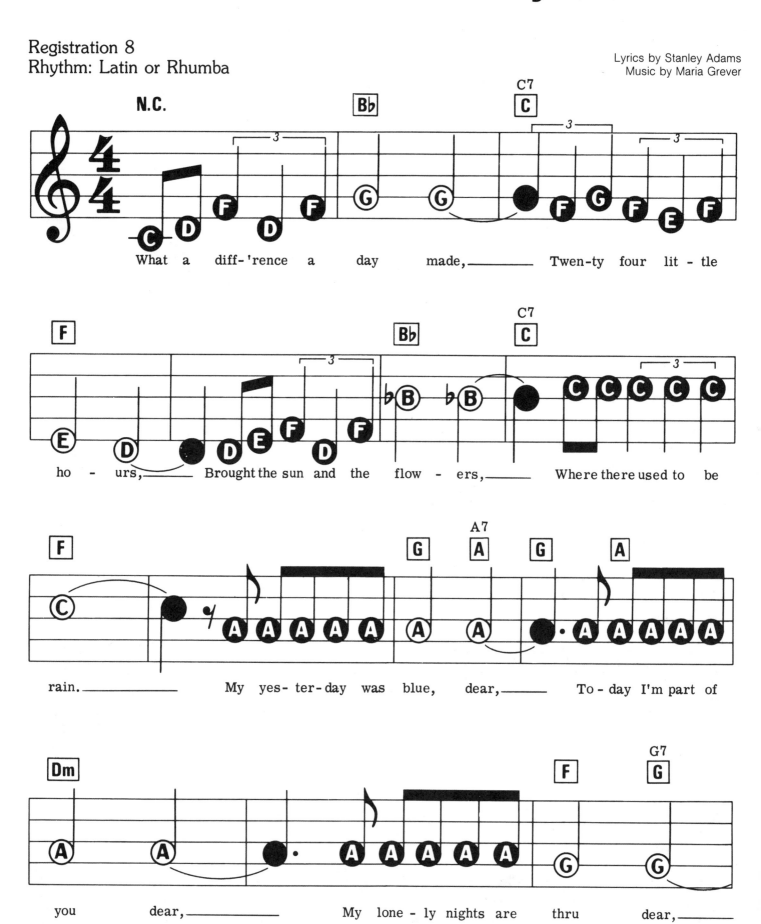

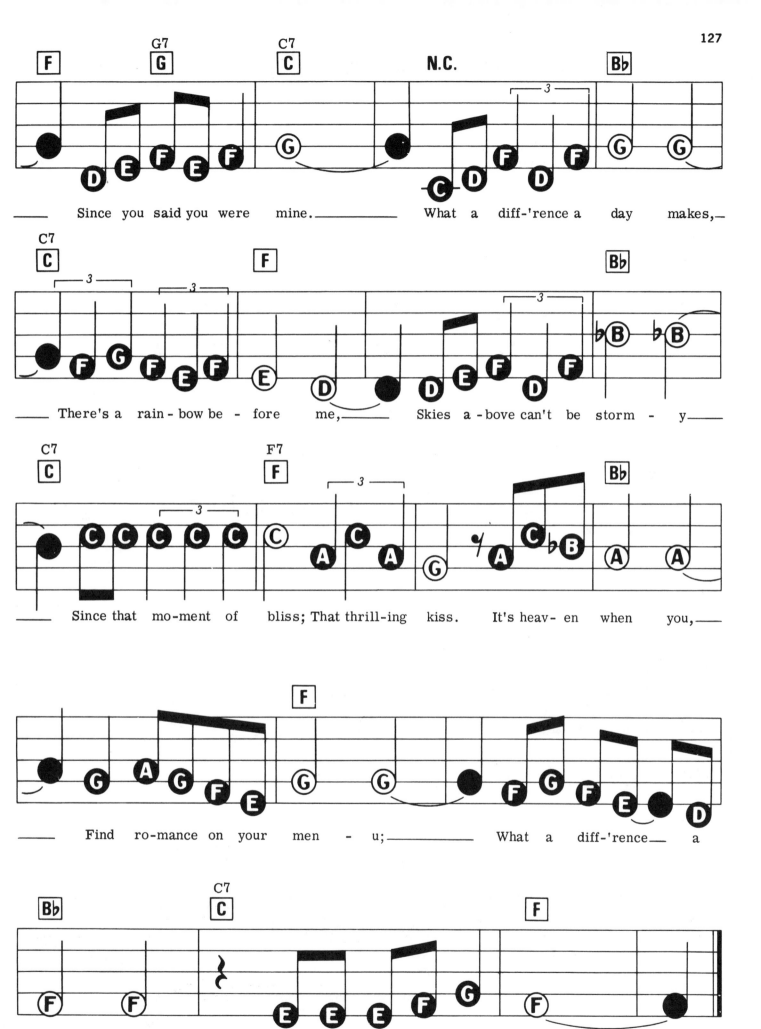

Where Or When

(From "BABES IN ARMS")

Registration 7
Rhythm: Fox Trot or Ballad

Words by Lorenz Hart
Music by Richard Rodgers

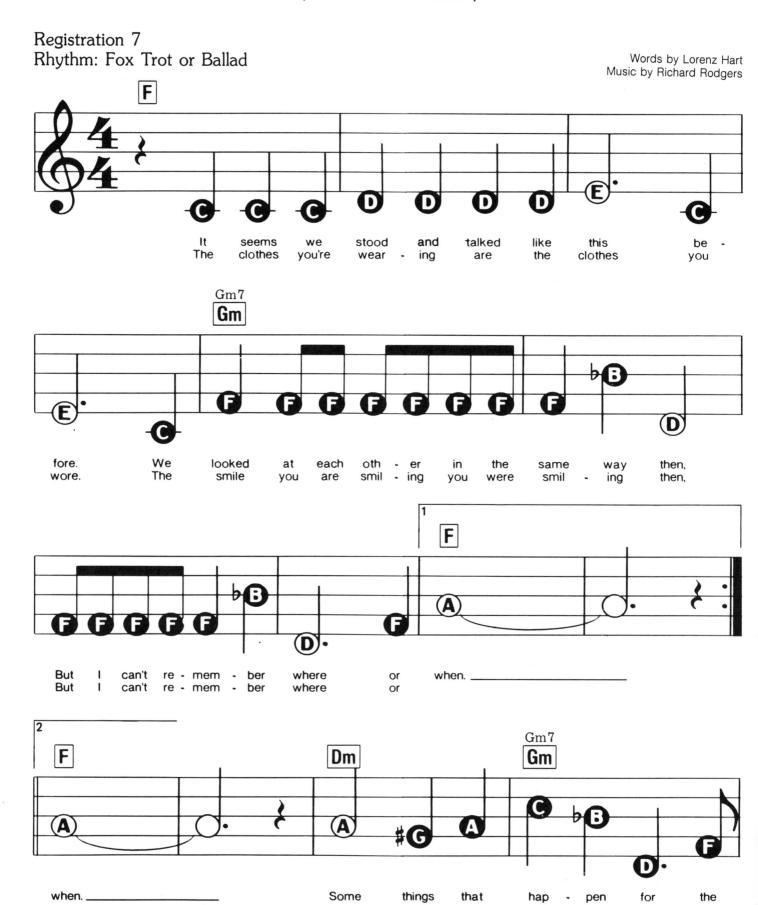

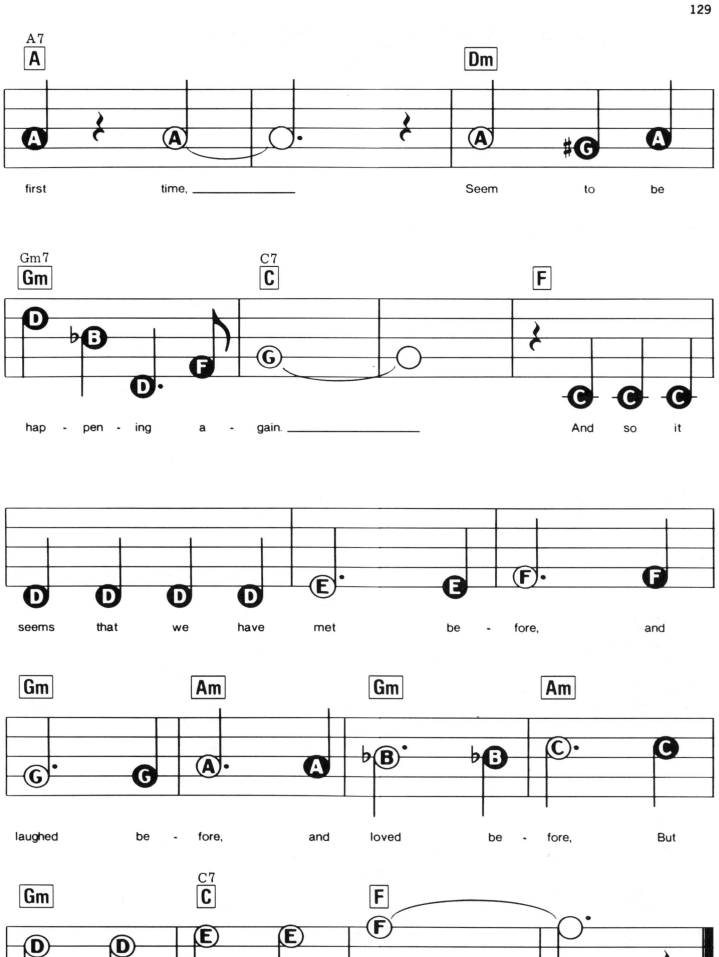

Where The Blue Of The Night
(Meets The Gold Of The Day)

Registration 1
Rhythm: Waltz

Words and Music by Fred E. Ahlert,
Bing Crosby and Roy Turk

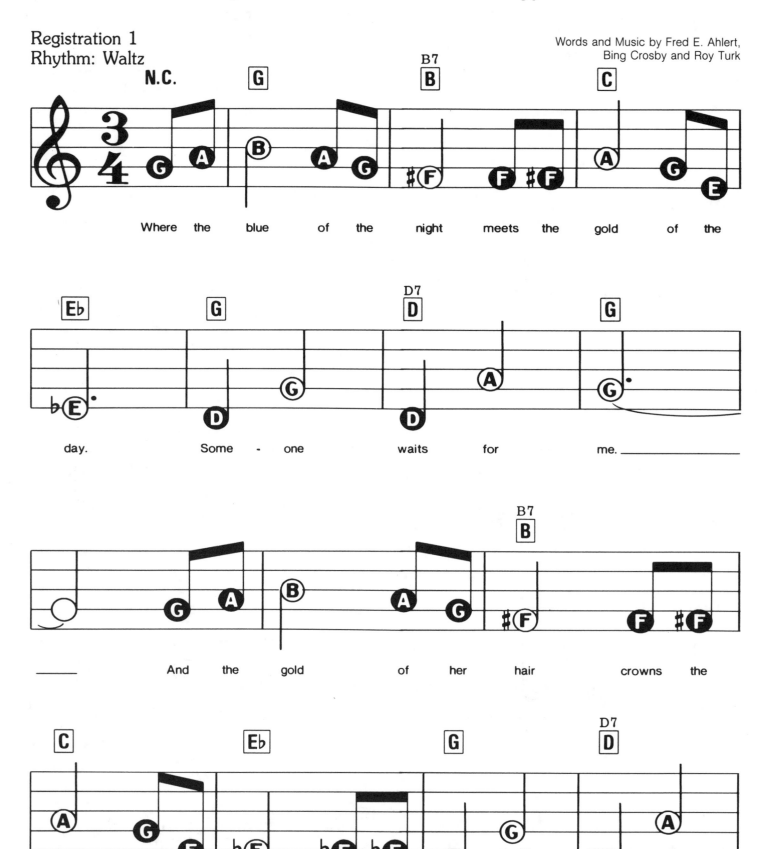

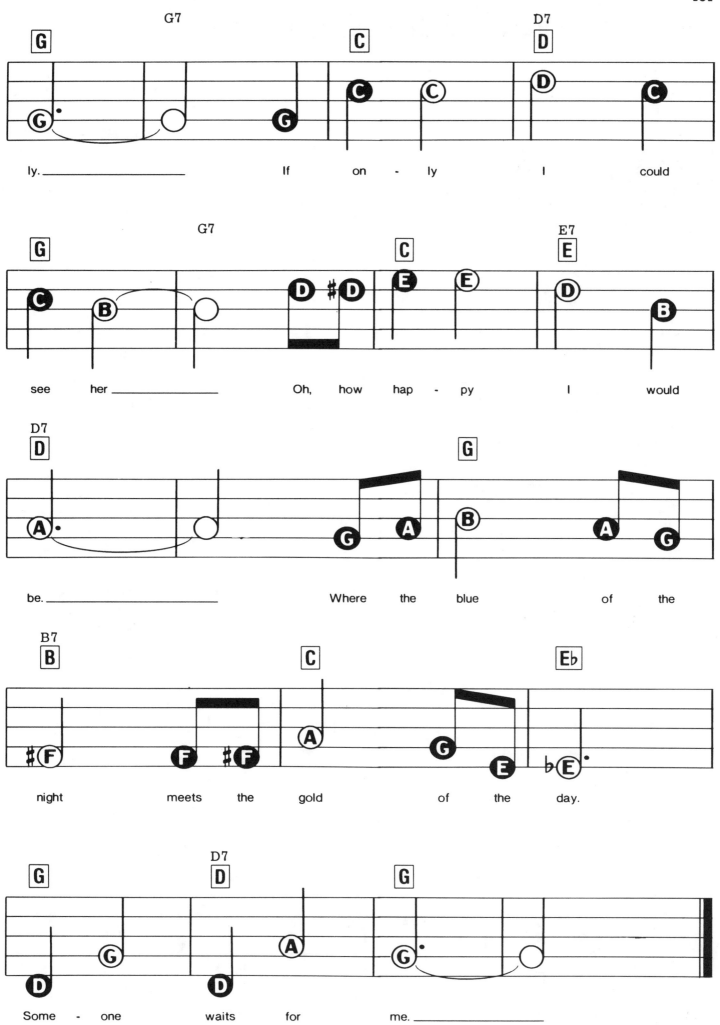

You're My Everything

Registration 3
Rhythm: Ballad or Jazz Rock

Words by Mort Dixon and Joe Young
Music by Harry Warren

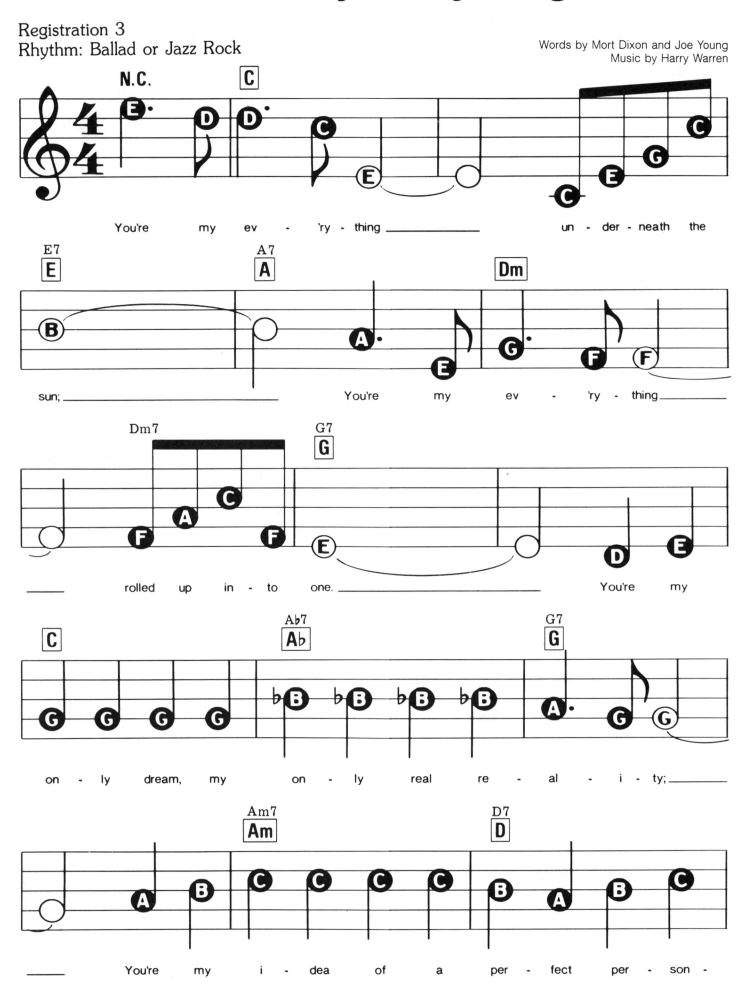

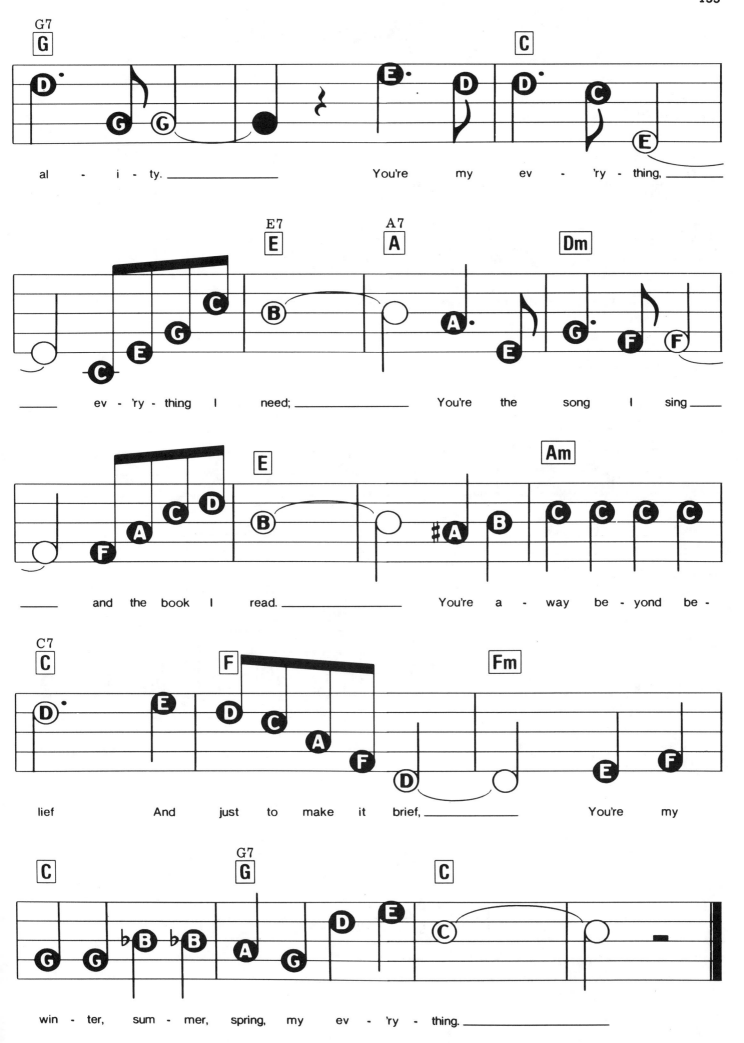

Yours

Registration 2
Rhythm: Rhumba or Latin

Words by Albert Gamse and Jack Sherr
Music by Gonzalo Roig

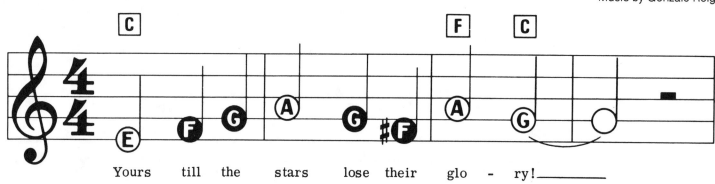

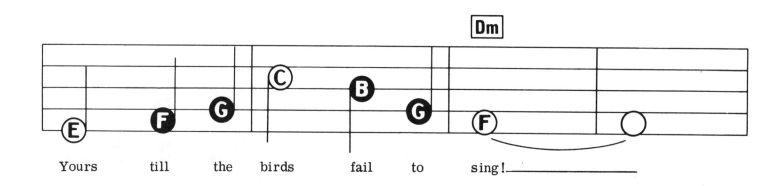

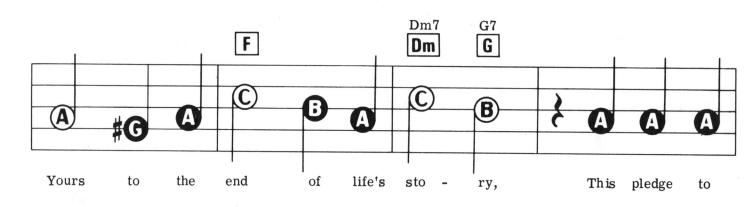

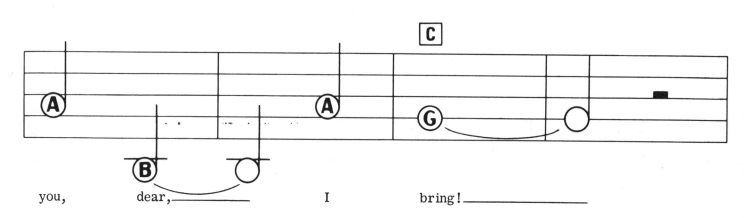

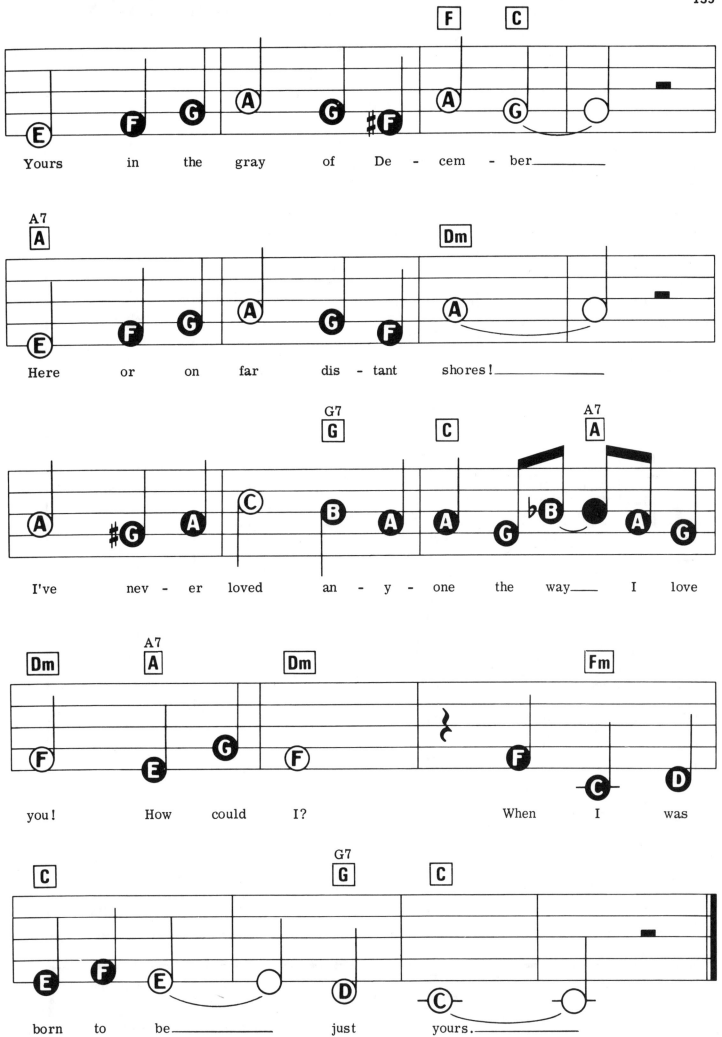

E-Z Play® TODAY Registration Guide
For All Organs

On the following chart are 10 numbered registrations for both tonebar (TB) and electronic tab organs. The numbers correspond to the registration numbers on the E-Z Play TODAY songs. Set up as many voices and controls listed for each specific number as you have available on your instrument. For more detailed registrations, ask your dealer for the E-Z Play TODAY Registration Guide for your particular organ model.

REG. NO.		UPPER (SOLO)	LOWER (ACCOMPANIMENT)	PEDAL	GENERALS
1	Tab	Flute 16', 2'	Diapason 8' Flute 4'	Flute 16', 8'	Tremolo/Leslie – Fast
	TB	80 0808 000	(00) 7600 000	46, Sustain	Tremolo/Leslie – Fast (Upper/Lower)
2	Tab	Flute 16', 8', 4', 2', 1'	Diapason 8' Flute 8', 4'	Flute 16' String 8'	Tremolo/Leslie – Fast
	TB	80 7806 004	(00) 7503 000	46, Sustain	Tremolo/Leslie – Fast (Upper/Lower)
3	Tab	Flute 8', 4', 2⅔', 2' String 8', 4'	Diapason 8' Flute 4' String 8'	Flute 16', 8'	Tremolo/Leslie – Fast
	TB	40 4555 554	(00) 7503 333	46, Sustain	Tremolo/Leslie – Fast (Upper/Lower)
4	Tab	Flute 16', 8', 4' Reed 16', 8'	Flute 8', (4) Reed 8'	Flute 8' String 8'	Tremolo/Leslie – Fast
	TB	80 7766 008	(00) 7540 000	54, Sustain	Tremolo/Leslie – Fast (Upper/Lower)
5	Tab	Flute 16', 4', 2' Reed 16', 8' String 8', 4'	Diapason 8' Reed 8' String 4'	Flute 16', 8' String 8'	Tremolo/Leslie
	TB	40 4555 554 Add all 4', 2' voices	(00) 7503 333	57, Sustain	
6	Tab	Flute 16', 8', 4' Diapason 8' String 8'	Diapason 8' Flute 8' String 4'	Diapason 8' Flute 8'	Tremolo/Leslie – Slow (Chorale)
	TB	45 6777 643	(00) 6604 020	64, Sustain	Tremolo/Leslie – Slow (Chorale)
7	Tab	Flute 16', 8', 5⅓', 2⅔', 1'	Flute 8', 4' Reed 8'	Flute 8' String 8'	Chorus (optional) Perc Attack
	TB	88 0088 000	(00) 4333 000	45, Sustain	Tremolo/Leslie – Slow (Chorale)
8	Tab	Piano Preset or Flute 8' or Diapason 8'	Diapason 8'	Flute 8'	
	TB	00 8421 000	(00) 4302 010	43, Sustain	Perc Piano
9	Tab	Clarinet Preset or Flute 8' Reed 16', 8'	Flute 8' Reed 8'	Flute 16', 8'	Vibrato
	TB	00 8080 840	(00) 5442 000	43, Sustain	Vibrato
10	Tab	String (Violin) Preset or Flute 16' String 8', 4'	Flute 8' Reed 8'	Flute 16', 8'	Vibrato or Delayed Vibrato
	TB	00 7888 888	(00) 7765 443	57, Sustain	Vibrato or Delayed Vibrato

NOTE: TIBIAS may be used in place of FLUTES. VIBRATO may be used in place of LESLIE.

KEYBOARD ALPHABETICAL SONGFINDER

Complete listing of over 3000 songs included in the E-Z Play TODAY Songbook Series, SOLO TODAY, ORGAN ADVENTURE, EASY ELECTRONIC KEYBOARD MUSIC and PORTABLE KEYBOARD MUSIC Series. Song titles are cross-referenced to the books in which they can be found.

Available free of charge from your local music store. Or, write to:

HAL LEONARD PUBLISHING CORP. P.O. Box 13819, Milwaukee, WI 53213

Ask for #90500057.